Namibia SPACE

CHRIS MARAIS JULIENNE DU TOIT

Namibia
SPACE

CHRIS MARAIS
JULIENNE DU TOIT

First published in 2006 by Struik Publishers
(a division of New Holland Publishing (South Africa) (Pty) Ltd)

Garfield House
86–88 Edgware Road
W2 2EA London
United Kingdom
www.newhollandpublishers.com

14 Aquatic Drive
Frenchs Forest
NSW 2086
Australia

Cornelis Struik House
80 McKenzie Street
Cape Town, 8001
South Africa
www.struik.co.za

218 Lake Road
Northcote, Auckland
New Zealand

New Holland Publishing is a member of Johnnic Communication Ltd

Copyright © 2006 in published edition: Struik Publishers
Copyright © 2006 in text: Chris Marais and Julienne du Toit
Copyright © 2006 in photographs: Chris Marais

Publishing manager: Dominique le Roux
Managing editor: Lesley Hay-Whitton
Project Co-ordinator: Samantha Fick
Design director: Bruce Henderson
Concept designer: Nicola Parker
Designer: Nicola Parker
Editor: Patricia Myers Smith
Proofreader: Roxanne Reid

Reproduction by Hirt & Carter Cape (Pty) Ltd
Printed and bound by Kyodo Printing Co (S'pore) Pte Ltd, Singapore

ISBN 1 77007 332 9 (9 781770 073326)

1 3 5 7 9 10 8 6 4 2

Log on to our photographic website www.imagesofafrica.co.za for an African experience.

AUTHORS' NOTE

The Beautiful Blonde

When we want to be free of city and cellphone, computers and crimewaves, we go to Namibia.

In this rowdy neighbourhood party called southern Africa, Namibia is known as 'the beautiful blonde'. South Africa is busy and kaleidoscopic, Madagascar is mystical, Malawi is a game of bao by the lakeside, Zambia is a lazy Luangwa Valley hippo, Lesotho is a horseman on a hill, Mozambique is a plate of steaming prawns in the markets of Maputo, and Botswana is a shy sitatunga hurtling through the shallows of the Delta.

But Namibia is pure, unadulterated space. And silence. And peace. And a chance to exhale. This vast blonde land has been luring adventurers and travellers and prospectors for centuries.

We went travelling through Namibia in the Spring of 2004 on a six-week journey from the Fish River Canyon in the south to the end of the Caprivi Strip up north. This is what we saw. This is our Namibia ...

Namibia Space is dedicated to Julienne's parents, Trudy Dickens and Pierre du Toit, and to Chris's brother Butch, who loves the road more than anyone else.

The authors would also like to pay tribute and give thanks to the Namibia Tourism Board, Wilderness Safaris Namibia and everyone in Namibia who welcomed them along the way.

Chris and Jules

CONTENTS

NAMIBIA AT LARGE

Simply *Mirabilis*

THE BLONDE LAND

ONCE YOU'VE BEEN AROUND NAMIBIA A COUPLE OF TIMES, YOU START RECOGNISING THE SAME OLD FACES, YEAR AFTER YEAR. WE CALL THEM 'SANDBOX ADDICTS', BECAUSE THEY SAVE ALL THEIR LEISURE TIME, THEIR SICK LEAVE, THEIR ANNUAL VACATIONS AND THEIR LONG WEEKENDS TO SLIP ACROSS THE BORDERS AND VISIT THEIR BELOVED BEST SPOTS. THEY'VE BASICALLY COME TO PLAY IN THE WORLD'S LARGEST SANDBOX: NAMIBIA.

The addicts arrive from South Africa, Germany, Switzerland, France and the USA. They also fly out from Japan, where space is tight. And once they're out here on the dunes, in the vastness, under a canopy of stars so close you feel you could pluck one from the midnight sky, they revel in this blonde wilderness.

The appeal of Namibia for travellers, especially overlanders with time on their side, is varied: there is history, there is close-up Nature, there is infinite sand shaped by constant wind, there are exotic people, many of whom have turned their backs on civilisation and still practise their old ways, there are great herds of animals – and there is The Road, with its infinite possibilities.

This is the land where the Bushmen still walk. Where the Basters migrated from the old Cape Colony and set up their stylish republic at Rehoboth. Where the Himba came over the Kunene River and set up home in the Kaokoveld, tending their herds of cattle and painting themselves with ochre and butterfat. Where their brothers moved south and became the Herero, taking on the dress of the old-time missionaries. Where the Ovambo and the Kavango lived off a great African river system and the Damara kept their own counsel in the mountains and the Nama trekked up from Namaqualand for their place in the sun.

And then, just before the end of the 19th century, this is where the German colonial forces came and set up shop. This is where diamond fields were discovered, so rich they had to be barred from the public eye, and prospectors made fortunes from little islands loaded with the bird guano so precious to the gardens of Europe. This country also has the Skeleton Coast, where dozens of passing ships ran aground and spewed forth survivors onto the beach, giving birth to legends both told and untold. Adventurers, hunters and Dorsland Trekkers passed through here on their way to other frontiers and left their marks – and often their very own bones – in the sand.

This is where, after independence in 1990, the fledgling tourism industry boomed into a serious threat to the eternal diamond for prime spot on the national earnings list. After the apartheid guns were stilled, new types of vehicles could be seen travelling on the shiny black roads once almost exclusively

Above: War as art – 'aero-crafts' on the B8 blacktop highway going north into the Kavango region, possibly inspired by the old military camps on the border.

Previous page: The great survivor of Namibia's desert plains: *Welwitschia mirabilis*.

used by the military. Overland trucks, bakkies and soft-shell hire cars appeared, full of dead-keen tourists who have never stopped coming back.

'I've been coming here for ten years, for six weeks at a time,' the Swiss dentist told us as he focused his long lens at an oryx slowly moving through the distant dunescape of Sossusvlei. 'I hope to come here for 20 more.'

All manner of tourists come to Namibia these days. The young, adventurous travellers with lean pockets come to ride the dunes on boards, on buggies and in huge balls, staying in backpackers' hostels and congregating at town laundrettes by night, living on breakfast bars and bottled water and spending all their money on jaunts and outings and special deals, getting the most out of their adrenaline ride.

Many of the older tourists travel in huge double-decker buses in great comfort and style, enjoying each other's company and the stick-to-the-ribs German cuisine on offer in the major centres.

More and more, you're finding international amateur photographic clubs coming out to Namibia, also travelling in packs, bearing very expensive equipment and falling to the ground for a 'belly safari' at the slightest provocation. For these guys, an hour spent photographing a lichen field in the Messum Crater can be just as rewarding as sitting by a water hole at rush hour up at the Etosha National Park. Photographic safaris are just perfect fits for the landscape, people and animals of Namibia, and it's amazing to see how much money is spent on photo-gear, binoculars and safari outfits.

Then you get your 'tourist twin-set', that loving couple travelling around the country in a hired car. They'll be staying at resorts, B&Bs, lodges, guest houses and hotels, keeping to the major roads and enjoying the full benefits of a road trip without too much equipment.

Of course, Namibia is also just right for 4x4 campers who like to chug out into a vast horizon in their bakkies packed with awesome tents, fishing rods, cooler systems and just about everything that opens and shuts. This type of tourist – mainly South African – has been the blessing and the bane of Namibia for decades. In many ways these 4x4 travellers have pioneered national tourism throughout Namibia, but they've also made too many unnecessary tracks into ecosensitive areas, leaving behind one too many beer bottles in the process. And out here in the Great Dry Namib a beer bottle can stand for many a decade as mute witness to humans' occasional inhumanity to the next travelling person.

But times are changing: legislation is tightening up and constant awareness campaigns are having a positive effect on tourists, who are now more committed to leaving a lighter environmental footprint on Namibia. – Chris

NAMIBIA: QUICK FACTS

Population:	1.8 million.
Languages:	English is the official language, but Afrikaans, German and a number of indigenous languages are also widely spoken.
Currency:	Namibian dollar (Nam$), equivalent to South African rand (also accepted as legal tender).
Climate:	Hot days, cold nights, low rainfall generally; further northeast, there is more rain and the vegetation is greener.
Capital:	Windhoek.
Economy:	The major generators of GDP are mining (mainly diamonds and uranium), agriculture and tourism.
Electricity:	220 volts, the same as South Africa; plug points are identical.
Size:	824 292 sq km – about twice the size of Zimbabwe.
Roads:	Most roads are excellent. The main roads converging on Windhoek are tarred and secondary roads with gravel surfaces are graded regularly, but it is generally good policy to be aware of wild animals, sudden curves and sharp stones in the road, especially at night.
Conservation:	Namibia was the first country in the world to include protection of the environment in its constitution. Nearly 16 per cent of the land is protected by National Parks legislation.
Special animals:	Look out for the rare, endemic black-faced impala in northwestern Namibia and the Damara dik-dik (both can be seen at Etosha), the desert-adapted elephant and the black rhino (best seen in the Kaokoveld). Namibia also has the world's largest population of endangered cheetahs.

Left: Art Nouveau home on the hill. **Below:** End of the line – Lüderitz Station. **Right:** Lone quiver tree in the southern canyonlands. **Bottom:** Meandering course of the ancient Fish River.

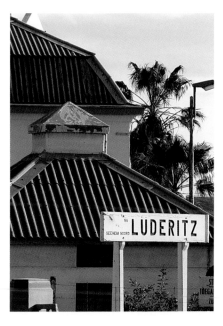

Opposite page – **Left:** Himba children on the Angolan border. **Top:** A southern Namibian shepherd on his early morning rounds. **Bottom:** Dinner at a Caprivi lodge.

This page – **Above:** Tourists have created quirky shapes with stones at the top of the Fish River Canyon. **Below:** One of the 'ghost mansions' of Kolmanskop, recently restored. **Right:** Full moon at Sossusvlei.

Above: Sunset at gecko level in the Namib. **Right:** One of the Big Brother classic dunes of Sossusvlei. **Below:** A tourist in his own creative space in the Dead Vlei.

Above: A quiver tree corridor outside Keetmanshoop. **Top right:** Solemn carvings stand guard at Otjikoto, the legendary bottomless lake. **Far right:** Deadwood – sun-bleached remains of a shipwreck on the Skeleton Coast. **Right:** Young upstanding member of the quiver tree tribe.

Fish River Canyon

THE LAND OF LOOK-AGAIN

THE FIRST TIME I CLIMBED OUT OF THE VEHICLE ON THE ROCKY ROAD TO AI-AIS IN THE FISH RIVER CANYON, THE SILENCE GREETED ME AS IF IT WERE A LIVING CREATURE. THIS SILENCE WAS A TOWERING, OVERWHELMING, SHIMMERING PRESENCE — THE COUNTERPOINT TO EVERYTHING I'D EVER HEARD. MY CITY-BRED EARS RANG WITH OUTRAGE AND BEWILDERMENT. WHAT WAS THIS VACUUM?

But over the next few days I found myself seeking out silence, relishing its sweet uncritical patience, and wondering how its absence unbalances us – like those children in Hong Kong one hears of who have never seen the horizon or the stars.

Of all Namibia's many dry spaces, the Fish River Canyon must be the most arid and, to the untrained eye, the most lifeless. The scouring desert wind can seem your only company.

But this, as I soon realised, was the land of look-again. At first, you are aware only of the elements: heat, rock, air. Then the corner of your eye might catch the swoop of a bird in flight, and your mind opens slowly to the possibility of life hidden among the rocks. You round a bend and chance upon two klipspringer, as delicately balanced on their tiny black hooves as ballerinas, calmly nuzzling a sage-green bush. Or you may glimpse a rock that turns into a lizard, or a baboon scrambling up the scree of a steep rock face. The natural hollows in the rocks become redefined as shelters for small creatures, dassie rats and rock rabbits, ground squirrels and adders.

If you want to be within walking distance of the canyon, the second-largest in the world after the Grand Canyon in Arizona, there are only two places to stay – the Ai-Ais resort, which is close to the riverbed and built around a hot mineral spring, or Hobas, a campsite close to the lip of the canyon, and the entry point for the 90-kilometre Fish River hiking trail.

Ai-Ais resembles a kind of convalescent's home from decades ago. Writer Lawrence G. Green says the water benefited paralysed children and sufferers of rheumatoid arthritis, many of whom were carried down to the hot springs on beds and later recovered full use of their limbs. He ascribed this to the theory that the water was radioactive and mineral rich. The latter may be true, but the former, thank goodness, is not. Green was writing at a time when people still believed that radioactivity was quite good for the system.

Before being the Lourdes of southern Africa, the water was used by the Nama people, who gave the springs their name (Ai-Ais means 'scalding hot') and then as a base by the German *Schutztruppe* at the beginning of the last century, when they were fighting the Nama.

We stayed at Ai-Ais, now a government-owned rest camp that feels like a time-trip back into the 1970s. A startling number of South African families come here every year, most of them staying in the fine

Above: Nestled into a rocky landscape in the Fish River Canyon area, Cañon Lodge is a traveller's oasis.

Previous Page: The majestic Fish River Canyon, second only in size to the Grand Canyon in the USA.

campsite. We met one on the spreading veranda, all of us drinking golden draughts of Namibia's finest to drown the dry, pervasive heat. The various parts of their clan are scattered between Johannesburg, Kimberley and Cape Town. So they all make an annual pilgrimage to Ai-Ais for a leisurely reunion.

We stayed on till late afternoon, when a breeze sprang up and lightly blew snatches of campsite conversation to us. The braai fires had been lit, and the happy campers were outside their tents, sipping Namib beer. Some of the more hardened sorts were getting into their G-and-Ts or brandy-and-Cokes as the aroma of seared meat rose into the canyon.

Three burly South African friends discussed favourite Namibian fishing spots. One hardy Brit couple working on their overland vehicle regaled an awestruck Windhoek woman with tales about their near-death experience at the hand of potential kidnappers in Brazzaville. At another braai fire, mothers with toddlers compared notes on how to keep dust out of the kitchen boxes. A huge German

overlanding double-trailer truck – Das Rollende Hotel – rumbled into the campsite, disgorging clots of chattering Germans. In the shop, an Italian family was doing some serious purchasing – wine, chips, chocolates. One member triumphantly hunted down the last two boxes of Eet Sum Mor biscuits. '*Brava, brava,*' her sister cheered. And through it all, a newly minted baby in her 4x4 all-terrain pram slept soundly in the cool canyon breeze.

Early the next morning, as recommended by the kind man at the reception desk, we headed off towards Hobas, intending to dangle our feet over the lip of the deep canyon and to appreciate the magnificent view over Hell's Bend.

An hour's slow drive later, as the heat, wind and dust were starting to build, we passed an unexpected billboard showing a gorgeous-looking old farmhouse surrounded by palm trees and flowers. The text promised accommodation, a restaurant, a swimming pool and horse riding at the Cañon Lodge. It seemed to advertise another planet. Further on, a sign indicated the Cañon Roadhouse. A roadhouse, here?

Unwavering, though, we headed on towards the canyon, its stark depths glimpsed here and there along the road. Finally, at the end of a stony track, we stopped at the view site of Hell's Bend, a gigantic, petrified switchback of an oxbow, which can be studied at length from the shade of a considerably built, open-walled shelter.

There are many view sites, but this is as good a point as any from which to gape at the great abyss. I could not believe that the demure, greenish line half a kilometre down had been capable of carving such a gigantic canyon for itself.

Writer and geologist Michael Brittan felt the same way, describing the Fish River, in his 1979 book *Discover Namibia*, as 'a shadow of its former fury, a fitful stream slumbering in the yawning trench of its own making'. He and other rock experts such as Nicole Grünert go on to explain it was not the Fish River alone that carved this enormous chasm, 550 metres deep, 161 kilometres long and 27 kilometres across at its widest point. There was a conspiracy of events. Its history started 350 million years ago with a fault line splitting open, continued with the river scouring away rock over millennia, and ended with a Gondwanaland glacier adding the finishing touches, cleaving through rocks more than a billion years old.

Says Brittan: 'The Fish River Canyon has a time-ravaged quality all of its own, born it seems of the tremendous age of its Archaean rocks which not even the Grand Canyon can match. In its frightening desolation and emptiness it stands alone. The surroundings too are parched, stark and silent – even botanical life hardly dares intrude. Few roads scar this wilderness. Here it is still possible to be utterly alone, unmolested by tourists and unfettered by amenities crowding the edge of the gorge.'

We drove further along the road parallel to the canyon and stopped at a little cityscape of cairns. At Rockies Point, it seemed a merry spirit had infected visiting tourists. On the very lip of the canyon, travellers have amused themselves by building little castles, Stonehenges, pyramids, pagodas, bridges, paths, faces and crucifixes. This was something more than people just passing the time; it was a thread of unconnected visitors, each one adding, with good humour, a little more to the efforts of previous ones. Tourists had made a tourist attraction. I'd never seen anything like it. Naturally we were overtaken by the urge ourselves – our two little towers lie between a pagoda and a bridge.

On our way back, we could not resist breakfast at the Cañon Roadhouse, which was like a kind of Baghdad Café in the middle of nowhere, a quirky place with reasonably priced accommodation and décor constructed from old farm implements, ploughs, retired petrol bowsers and scrapped artefacts. In the yard, cacti grew from the chassis of ancient vehicles and loungers lay around a sparkling blue pool that had been a farm dam in a previous life.

The four Cañon properties (the Roadhouse, Village, Mountain Camp and Lodge) constitute the happy ending to a sad story that started a hundred years ago. Two brothers, Alfons and Stefan Schanderl, came out from Germany and built a prosperous farm here at the beginning of the twentieth century. They were broken-hearted at being forced to abandon it years later during the First World War. This property now falls within the privately owned, 100 000-hectare nature reserve called Gondwana Cañon Park, created in 1996. It adjoins the 345 000-hectare government conservation area encompassing the canyon. The new owners, under a company called Nature Investments, have vowed to 'Give back to Nature what belongs to

Nature' and are restoring the land to its former wild self. They also have a self-sufficiency project, in the spirit of the Schanderl brothers, and supply guests with fresh herbs, vegetables, milk, eggs, home-made breads, salamis and bacon.

Curious, we visited the Cañon Village, which resembled the empty set of a cowboy film. The guests had all gone off for a horse ride to the canyon and the friendly staff showed us around. The walls of the dining room are covered with a painted mural history of the Bondelswart Nama people.

We also stopped at the Cañon Lodge we had seen on the billboard. Entranced at how hospitable it looked, we wandered up to the restaurant area. Through the windows we saw the kitchen staff preparing *frikkadelle* (rissoles) for lunch. Quite unselfconsciously, they launched into a spontaneous and perfectly harmonised hymn, 'Amazing Grace'. It was one of those flawless moments that just seem to happen in the generous space a desert offers, so natural that the visitors sitting at the tables hardly raised their heads from writing postcards.   – Julie

Above and right: The well and the painting (a series of murals) are found inside the restaurant of the Cañon Village. The well is a replica of an old-time water-well in Namibia, while the mural depicts the war between Germans and Nama in the early 1900s.

Opposite page – **Top left:** The entrance to the A1-Ais resort. **Top right:** Rock cairns left by tourists moving through the canyon. **Bottom left:** Quiver tree landscape of rock and scrub. **Bottom right:** A klipspringer browsing on twigs in the canyon.

This page – **Above:** A scrap car transformed into a plant box. **Right, top:** A farm dam becomes an inviting swimming pool. **Right, centre:** The alluring sign to the Cañon Lodge near the Fish River Canyon. **Right, bottom:** Township at Noordoewer on the border with South Africa.

KEETMANSHOOP

Sunset Forests

QUIVER-TREE COUNTRY

LEAVING THE DEEP CANYON OF THE FISH AND ITS ROCKY KINGDOMS, HEADED EAST FOR THE BLACKTOP COMFORT OF THE B1 HIGHWAY, DON'T BE SURPRISED IF YOU FIND YOURSELF FLOATING INTO A LOW-LYING BANK OF PINK CLOUD — AN EARLY MORNING DREAM STATE.

Add this to your southern Namibian experience: a three-pack of hectic German polkas on the radio, conjuring up those 'flaxen girls' who were occasionally spotted in the beer halls of German South West outposts; a passing parade of drought-tortured quiver trees and sage-green milkbushes; a herd of Nguni cattle making angry eye-contact in the mist.

And to top it all off, here comes a young Nama shepherd on his rattletrap bicycle, loudly marshalling his band of Dorpers across the dirt road. As a backdrop, the shepherd has a series of cone-shaped mountains with trees climbing up their flanks like British soldiers on assault manoeuvres. Those are the Klein Karasberge, distant whalebacks coming and going in the milky visibility of the day.

You pass a squarely built, whitewashed farmhouse with no frills attached – except, of course, for a satellite dish sticking out on one side.

'Yep, I knew it,' I say to Jules.

'What?'

'A bachelor farmer lives here.'

'How can you tell?'

'Easy. No garden. No fancy curtains in the windows. Lots of TV channels to choose from – especially sport.'

We drive on. Sometimes it's more fun to speculate on the nature of people and things without actually meeting them and possibly being disappointed. An axe-murdering granny might be living in that little white blockhouse, and then where would my theory be?

'Explain. Does that mean she murders axes? Or that she uses axes to commit her crimes?'

'OK. Let's just say chances are excellent a bachelor lives there …'

We swing back onto the tarmac, the black, winding B1 snake heading north to Keetmanshoop. Just over the Gamkab River, I stop and take photographs of windpumps and a farm dam – the archetypal Dry Land Kodak moment available from the Karoo to the Kalahari to the Karasberge and beyond.

In the sleepy settlement of Grünau we meet the Christiaan family, descendants of the fierce Nama leader Hendrik Witbooi, who led a highly effective guerrilla war against the German colonials just after the 20th century kicked off.

These days, however, the Christiaan family just prays for work to arrive from somewhere. Occasionally it does, in the form of a farmer from South Africa needing 'seasonals' to pick fruit south of the border along the Gariep River. Sometimes there is a job available at the Rosh Pinah mine.

'But it's mostly piece-work,' says Jims 'Six' Christiaan. 'We live in a desert cage here.'

We drive on, towards Keetmanshoop, listening to Namibian radio offerings. On 106.5 FM, Damara-Nama Radio, we can't understand the clicks, the sing-song tones and the harsh glottals, but it all sounds wonderful. Perhaps this is how it was when the night fires were lit out on the desert and the First People gathered for a feast and a bit of a trance dance until the shaman's nose bled and people began seeing apparitions leaping out of the flames.

Just outside Keetmanshoop, we fill the bakkie at the Lafenis Lodge and change the radio station to NBC, where Eric Clapton and Cream are performing 'Sunshine of Your Love'. The motto at the Lafenis Lodge proclaims: 'Where the modern meets the old wild west.'

Don't pass through Keetmanshoop without visiting its Quiver Tree Forest, on the farm of Coenie and Ingrid Nolte. We pay our twenty Nambucks and walk through a stand of quiver trees in the late afternoon light. Their leaves are bronze, their stems gold as they stand there rooted in the lemon grass and black iron rocks.

We drive on to the Giant's Playground, a confusing world of jumbled stones balanced precariously on one another. Jules loses the car keys for a while and we really get to explore the place. She says a fervent prayer to St Anthony (Finder of car keys? Protector of those who lose car keys?) and discovers them in the twilight. Which is good, because I had not looked forward to bedding down here amongst the behemoth rocks for the night.

In the morning, we join most of Keetmanshoop at the railway station to welcome Union Limited Steam Rail Tours, which has arrived with 600 tonnes of heaving, blowing steel in the form of two 19D locos. Oh, those good old sooty days!

Above: Quiet church scene in the desert town of Grünau, on the way north to Keetmanshoop.
Previous Page: Sunset at the Quiver Tree Forest outside Keetmanshoop.

Whenever a cross-country steam locomotive pulls into an outback town – anywhere in the world – the metal giant and its passengers are given the regal treatment by the locals. There is much gawking and admiration, and the strolling passengers all take on an air of ownership about their train. They're moving on, in grand style, in a huge wheeled ship through the desert. The people of Keetmanshoop, however, stoically return to their daily duties.   – Chris

Left: Namibian road travel – one of southern Africa's great tourism experiences. **Top:** The enigmatic Karasberge line up along the B1 Highway. **Above:** Hardy Dorper sheep are farmed in the southlands.

Left and bottom left: One of Namibia's great survivors – the quiver tree. **Below:** Natural stone formations at the Giant's Playground outside Keetmanshoop. **Right:** Expert stonemasonry of the Rhenish Mission Society Church in Keetmanshoop. **Bottom right:** Water well outside the church, where visitors can see how locals drank before the time of taps and pipes.

Lüderitz

Angra Pequena

THE FIRST FRONTIER

DRIVING WEST FROM KEETMANSHOOP, WE CROSS A SERIES OF DRY RIVERS CALLED THE NAIAMS, THE SCHNEPFEN AND THE GURIB UNTIL WE COME TO A MOUNTAIN CALLED DIK WILLEM. WE DROP OFF THE MAIN ROAD AT THE VILLAGE OF AUS BECAUSE THE OLD WRITERS SPEAK OF AUS AS A 'MOUNTAIN VILLAGE WITH THE FAINT ATMOSPHERE OF SWITZERLAND'. THIS, OUT HERE IN THE SOUTHERN NAMIB, WE SIMPLY HAVE TO SEE.

There's not much to yodel about as we drive into Aus in search of the legendary Bahnhofs Hotel, once described as an 'Alpine inn'. We find Edition Three of the hotel (its predecessors burnt down) and it declares 'we are tourist friendly' in a sign on the stoep.

The Grillenbergers arrive by the time Round Two of the Aus Village Tafel Lager Drink-Up has commenced. We are outside where once world travellers and soldiers may have sat, marvelling at the utter 'Swissness' of Aus. To us, however, it looks like a typical tiny desert settlement where nothing much happens, definitely not great for a fondue club, but very amiable nevertheless. And the beers are cheap.

Karl Grillenberger was born here more than fifty years ago, in the Roman Catholic Mission church clinic. He grew up on a nearby farm, high-schooled in Lüderitz and ended up a successful man in Cape Town. He is back on a Memory Lane trip.

'Nothing's changed,' says Karl, gazing out at the main street.

'Everyone seems so poor,' says his wife Joan, who is still in two minds about this grand Namibian odyssey. 'But somehow they look quite happy.'

'That's the point,' says Karl. 'There are no rich people living around here to make them feel poor.' Food for thought, indeed…

Just after Aus the vegetation changes, opening up with lower, dark mountains and drifting sands. Not more than 20 kilometres on at Garub, we come across 18 wild horses nibbling at sand and stone at the roadside. Although some have battle limps and bear signs of hard living, these legendary wild horses of the Namib are well muscled and alert. A half-grown colt is shadowed by its indulgent black dam. Two chestnuts nuzzle one another in secret discourse.

A Pajero packed with Gauteng trippers comes screaming over the horizon. You can smell brake pads burning as they narrowly avoid colliding with a brace of stallions. The driver honks his horn impatiently as they cross, then fires up first gear and blasts his way to Lüderitz.

'Maybe they've been here before,' I say in their defence. 'Maybe they're used to seeing the horses.'

'Or maybe they wouldn't know a special sight if it came up and bit them,' says my wife. 'Did you notice the plates?'

'Yeah, they're from Gauteng. Just like us …'

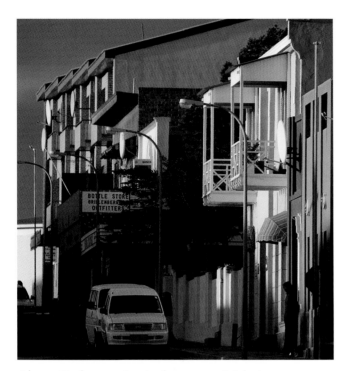

Above: Early morning in downtown Lüderitz.
Previous page: The Lutheran Felsenkirche, the most recognizable landmark in Lüderitz.

Lots of things prepare you for the faraway experience of Lüderitz. There's Aus, there are the wild horses of the Namib, there's even an old one-horned gemsbok rooting around near the ghost town of Kolmanskop – your very own unicorn, if you have a romantic heart.

Then there's the wind, a dragon of a southwester that could whip you off your feet if you were a little light on them to begin with. That wind has also been bringing diamonds in from the sea for millions of years, but more of that in a while.

As you drive through the crescent-shaped dunescapes to the coast, you encounter a place that looks like a set from *Toy Story*. In a base of pastel desert, the *Jugendstil* (Art Nouveau) houses are blue and red and white up there on the Diamantberg, where the Gothic old Felsenkirche looms over the town.

We arrive at The Nest, the finest hotel in Lüderitz, where we are given a film-star suite with the waves literally lapping at the patio base. The ebullient Ulf Grunewald, manager and part-owner, has organised us a ridiculously low rack rate and, after a fortnight of roughing it in sand and rock, we sink with gratitude into the delights of the Cormorant Suite.

'Not bad for a pair of skanky desert rats,' says Jules, as we tip half the Kalahari and a chunk of the Namib from our boots out into the Atlantic Ocean...

A brief rundown on Lüderitz:

In 1883 a German merchant called Adolf Lüderitz sent Heinrich Vogelsang down to these parts to establish a trading relationship with the local tribes. By then a sailor called David Radford had already settled in what was known as Angra Pequena with his wife – subsequently they had eight children. Radford and his family collected shark oil, fish and sealskins for trade with the markets in Cape Town.

Vogelsang bought the bay from the local chief Josef Fredericks from Bethanie for 100 pounds and 200 rifles – with accessories. A year later, it was declared a German Protectorate. An initially spurned Radford was given a life annuity for having been there in the first place, and Angra Pequena was renamed Lüderitz.

Thus, from this little coastal spot on the Atlantic seaboard, began the grand German occupation of what is today called Namibia. For more than 30 years, the German flag flew over the South West – with disastrous results for the indigenous tribes. And when the South African government took over after the First World War, it pursued the German policies with a matched vigour.

Back in Lüderitz, however, no one noticed that they were literally walking on a vast bed of super-grade diamonds until 1907, when a railroad labourer made a spectacular find near Kolmanskop. This led to a crazy, colourful, champagne-swilling, caviar-scoffing era in which vast mansions were built into the rocks of the Diamantberg and men lay on the moonlit sands of the Namib, stuffing the glinting precious stones into their pockets and, sometimes, their mouths. The diamonds of Kolmanskop may be all gone now, but the Sperrgebiet (forbidden area) still protects those that remain on either side of the town.

The person to talk to about Lüderitz is Marion Schelkle, who runs Lüderitz Tours and Safaris from her office in the midtown area. Marion is a third-generation *Buchter* (which, loosely translated, means 'bay person') and grew up running barefoot in a tiny town that seemed to be caught in time – and growing rustier by the year.

In the 1970s, Lüderitz had reached its low point. There were fewer than six thousand residents left, with half the shops standing empty.

'The new boom began with the town's centenary in 1983,' says Marion. 'Everyone who'd ever been to Lüderitz came to see it breathe one last time. Then UNTAG (United Nations officials) arrived in 1989 to oversee the elections and gave the local economy a massive boost.'

After independence, many investments flowed in: fishing plants, a revived diamond-mining operation, gas mining and a whole new form of money-spinner – tourism.

'What about this wind?' we ask. 'Do you ever get used to it?'

She welcomes the challenge with a combative look in her eye: 'Firstly, there are far windier places in the world. Secondly, we arrange our activities around it. The tours to Kolmanskop are in the mornings, when there is less wind. The wind comes up in the afternoon and wipes out the tourist footprints of the morning – the next day it looks like an untouched ghost town again.

'When Mozambique was hit by floods in 1999, the wind stopped in Lüderitz for 19 days straight. We cried for the wind. It not only keeps the temperatures down, it pumps oxygen into the sea. The crayfish and other marine life suffered and died.

'As for getting used to it, my father used to say it's only the first 30 years that are the hardest…'

It's Heroes' Day in Namibia and the air in Lüderitz is dead still. Hardly a breeze in the streets. We take the Dias Cross loop drive and photograph colonies of flamingos dancing in the mud, teasing breakfast out of the black stuff.

We return at lunchtime to find Lüderitz in a dozy idyll, wind-free and peaceful. Out at Shark Island, we photograph a rather startled-looking resemblance of Adolf Lüderitz on a brass plaque. A century ago, more than a thousand interned Nama men, women and children died here as the result of conditions in the German prisoner-of-war camp, which earned the place the name of Death Island. Today, it's a campground with the best sea views in southern Africa.

The next morning we leave Lüderitz before the break of dawn. At Garub, we turn off to the water hole and have an exclusive breakfast with our new friends, the wild horses. Their leader, a watchful Palomino stallion, allows us to drift near the herd and take photographs. Then, when they've posed for us and drunk their fill, they disappear back into the mystical desert from whence they came.

Even if you only do it once in your lifetime, you have to see the world of Lüderitz, that faraway place at the end of the dunefields by the sea.   – Chris

Left: A seaside shanty reminiscent of the Scottish Hebrides. **Above:** *Jugendstil* (Art Nouveau) architecture became prevalent in Lüderitz between 1890 and 1920. **Below:** Flamingos are often found in the saline pans around Lüderitz. They are opportunists, seeking out places where rains have fallen, moving to the coast when inland waters dry up during winter.

Above left: The boardwalk to the Bartholomeu Dias Memorial. **Above:** The famous Goerke Haus in Lüderitz, most prominent of the town's 'diamond palaces'. **Left:** Adolf Lüderitz, trader and founder of the town named after him.

'What about the wind?' we ask. 'As my father used to say, it's only the first 30 years that are the hardest...'

Left: The guest house at Shark Island. **Above:** Part of the Lüderitz fishing fleet. **Bottom left:** A fishing boat moored and ready for another day at sea. **Below:** The waters off Lüderitz are some of the richest fishing grounds in the world.

Above left: The exterior detail on many old Lüderitz houses has been preserved. **Above:** Out of the wind – the courtyard of The Nest Hotel. **Left:** Stark rock formations on the Lüderitz peninsula. **Below:** A replica of the famous padrão (stone memorial) left by Bartolomeu Dias.

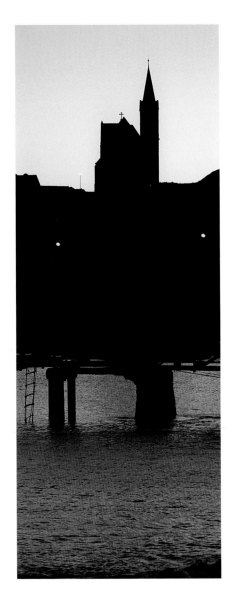

Above left: The Felsenkirche in sunset silhouette. **Above right:** Early morning flamingos feeding along the coastline.

We take the Dias Cross loop drive and photograph colonies of flamingos dancing in the mud, teasing breakfast out of the black stuff.

KOLMANSKOP

Wind and Sand

DIAMONDS IN THE DESERT

IT'S EARLY MORNING IN THE NAMIB DESERT AND THE AIR TASTES LIKE CHAMPAGNE, ONLY CLEANER AND WITH FEWER BUBBLES UP THE NOSE. A CHILL SLIDES DOWN THE BACK OF MY JERSEY AS I LIE ON THE SAND, LINING UP THE CAMERA LENS WITH A BROKEN-DOWN SECTION OF ANCIENT RAILWAY TRACK. THE RAILS SEEM TO RUN MADLY OVER THE HORIZON OF HISTORY AND BACK INTO THE DAYS OF GERMAN OCCUPATION, DIAMOND MOGULS AND SIMPLE EXPLORERS WHO ADORED THESE DRY LANDS. A CENTURY LATER, IT IS MY TURN TO PAY THEM HOMAGE.

Somewhere around here, between the hamlet of Aus and the coastal jewel of Lüderitz, August Stauch settled into a life of sand and rail and endless sky. What a change it must have been for the young German. He'd been building railway systems up in Pomerania when, like so many Victorian-era types from the First World, he was overcome by the dreaded asthma. And so, as was the custom, he applied for a posting in a hot climate. And they sent him to South West, Germany's finest colonial treasure, to make sure the endless Namib sands stayed off the precious railway tracks.

I've just been to Stauch's old place, a godforsaken little railway siding called Grasplatz, where the wind howls like a mad woman and the oryx walk with their heads down to avoid getting sand in their eyes. He must have had really bad lungs to give up the *Bierstuben* and lusty babes of Pomerania for this.

But maybe Stauch knew something the rest of the world only suspected, because he told his workers to keep a sharp eye out for strange stones, especially those very hard, glinty ones.

On a day in April 1908, the trusty Zacharias Lewala approached his boss with a couple of likely diamonds he'd found while clearing the line. Stauch tested them on the face of his watch and, like good diamonds everywhere, they simply sliced through the glass.

What happens after this to Messrs Lewala and Stauch? Of Zacharias we hear no more. August, according to the stories, makes a fortune and then loses it all somehow. Does he return to his little station at Grasplatz? No one can tell me.

The important element in all of this is that their discovery sparked off a fantastical diamond boom, with the little village of Kolmanskop as the epicentre. Up and down the coast from here, people found diamonds, literally just lurking in the sand. All they had to do, in many cases, was bend down and pick them up. Some workers carried them about in their mouths when their pockets flowed over. Others harvested them by the light of a full moon, when they shone at their best. What a time that must have been.

'Suddenly, it was almost as though it had rained diamonds overnight,' said the late travel writer T.V. Bulpin.

These were not the diamonds of Kimberley, embedded in blue stone and often only of industrial quality. These were mostly gem-standard diamonds, small and honed down and worked by the waters of the Orange River (formerly Gariep, then Orange, now Gariep again), dumped down at its mouth at Oranjemund, carried north by the currents and swept by wind onto the desert sands of Namibia. What a fabled river journey for a gemstone...

Kolmanskop – we had seen the photographs. That lonely old mansion on a hill of sand, faded and redolent of ancient evenings around the pianola, imported wines, starched collars, magical dishes whipped up out of nowhere, little girls in pinafores, German *Schutztruppe* in high boots, their horses safe in nearby stables, a brave patch of garden struggling outside in the arms of the Namib, a bag of diamonds lying open and glistening on the dinner table.

We finally get to see the Village of Sand, and although they've painted the 'icon house' back in its original colours, it still stands ghostly in the light of evening. We have to visit this place. So off we go to Kolmanskop's livelier neighbour, Lüderitz, to get the permits. Lüderitz also felt the hot breath of diamond frenzy back then.

'Beer halls, hotels and shops sprang up in the feverish, reckless atmosphere of this new El Dorado. Flaxen barmaids arrived. Over all floated the German eagle. Within a few years, the little group of huts had become the well-built town you see today. When there was a water shortage, people washed in imported soda water.' So says Lawrence G. Green, Bulpin's legendary forerunner in the travel-writing arena of southern Africa. And when our Mr Green speaks of the arrival of 'flaxen barmaids', you know he's talking about the Mother of all Parties.

Above: Ghost rail tracks cross the sands surrounding Kolmanskop.
Previous page: Young visitors play among the ruins at the ghost town of Kolmanskop.

There was a factory that supplied free ice – half a block a day to each household – lemonade and soda water. More than a thousand tons of water was shipped in from Cape Town each month.

'When the ship was delayed, they made their coffee from soda water,' says Ute Manns, our guide through the ghost town. 'They could buy more than their allotted 20 litres of water, but it was the same price as imported champagne.'

The factory used imported ammonia gas and electricity to cool seawater down and freeze fresh water in moulds. The butcher built his cold room next to the ice factory and thus had access to chilled pipes. Fans blew the cold air onto the carcasses. Next door was a bakery, which supplied each household with fresh, hot rolls each morning.

'And even though the water was so expensive,' says Ute, 'the miners cultivated extravagant gardens, many of them supplying places like Oranjemund with cut flowers.'

The shopkeeper was very wealthy, because the miners often paid for their groceries with diamonds. In her house stands an interesting-looking hat stand, and Jules asks Ute about it.

'That came from the first brothel in nearby Lüderitz,' she says. 'In those days, any transport rider who escaped being killed or kidnapped by Namas between Keetmanshoop and Lüderitz was received like a hero in the brothel. His tired feet were washed in imported champagne, and he was offered the pick of the girls.'

The Lüderitz brothel's madam was also very wealthy, it is said. She was paid in diamonds as well. She hoarded her diamonds under false floorboards in her dog's kennel. One day the *Schutztruppe* arrived, randy and remorseless. There was an argument about payment. The soldiers were never as good value as the miners, so the madam threw them out. In revenge, they almost shook her bungalow to pieces and were going to roll it down Diamantberg when she relented and let them in.

Kolmanskop had a very large hospital that could handle more than 200 patients. It had the first X-ray machine in southern Africa, and two most eccentric doctors. A Dr Kraenzle used to give every patient French champagne and caviar sandwiches in the belief that this was the ultimate distraction against pain. The other medico, Dr V. Lossow, used to eat a freshly chopped-up onion every morning, whistling a strange tune as he chewed it. It gave him such an immense feeling of wellbeing that he prescribed the same (including the Pythonesque singing ritual) to all his patients.

But you could be a strange doctor, a whoring colonial soldier or a person who grows exotic flowers in the desert out here. This was Kolmanskop, where, in less than two years, more than a million carats of diamonds were retrieved from leopard-crawling across the sands. Wads of money were thrown away at the horse races and men drank champagne out of women's shoes every night.

They staged fancy dances, masked balls, operettas and plays in a beautifully designed recreation hall, and the *Buchters* of Lüderitz, perhaps a little jaded by the bawdy goings-on up on Diamantberg, used to flock out into the desert for a night out in Kolmanskop. Life here was tough, colourful, interesting and, on a medical diet of champagne and caviar, more than a little toxic.   – Chris

The diamond-fuelled glory of Kolmanskop is gradually being swallowed by the dunes.

Top left: Stacked mountains lead the way into Lüderitz from the east. **Above:** The wind and sand are taking their toll on the Kolmanskop buildings. **Far left:** Heat and wind have warped the old Lüderitz–Keetmanshoop line. **Left:** Tourist tracks are wiped away overnight by the 'wind janitor'.

This page. Below: In its heyday, Kolmanskop had lush 'imported' gardens.
Right: A lookout into the desert lands.

Opposite page. Left: The windy road of drifting sands between
Keetmanshoop and Lüderitz. **Right:** Was there outdoor bathing out here a
century ago?

This was Kolmanskop, where, in less than two years, more than a million carats of diamonds were retrieved by leopard-crawling across the sands.

GARUB

Desert Herds

WILD HORSES

JULES AND I HUDDLED IN A WOODEN HIDE AT THE GARUB WATER HOLE BETWEEN LÜDERITZ AND KEETMANSHOOP AND AWAITED THE ARRIVAL OF THE LEGENDARY WILD HORSES OF THE NAMIB. I SET UP MY CAMERAS IN THE PREDAWN GLOAMING AND WE DRANK SOME COFFEE FROM A FLASK.

First light arrived and lit the desert in rich caramel tones. To the west, a rolling bank of low-lying mist retreated before the sun. Ten minutes later, the landscape turned to yellow sand plains rimmed by purple and black jagged mountains.

Because the horses drink only every 30 hours in summer and every 72 hours in cold weather, there was no guarantee they would grace us with their presence. But then we got lucky.

The horses began appearing in single file from the west, the east and the mountain range in the north – all converging on the water hole. A large troop of 17 arrived in orderly fashion, led by a powerful stallion in a golden palomino coat. His mares and foals – including one freshly born fuzzy colt with blonde streaks mixed into his dark mane hairs – lowered their heads into the water and drank as he watched, completely aware of our presence.

In the approach, each troop diffidently stood off a little before coming forward, as if observing some ancient dry-lands protocol. The horses snorted and nickered to each other, ears pricked forward, sharing the previous night's news. They drank their fill and stood in each other's shade, heads down and eyes half-closed, perhaps waiting to enter a far-off world of dreams where the grass grew like Christmas. Some mouthed the dung of others.

The wind had given many of the horses magnificent, flowing mane-dreadlocks. The young ones indulged in horseplay, chewing their friends' manes and nuzzling their withers, rolling their eyes in mock outrage. Soon there were more than 40 desert horses before us, totally involved in their post-dawn rituals. We were in the very midst of a personal 'breakfast session' of wild and legendary Namib horses.

By 2004, about 140 horses were living in the ancient Namib, having been completely independent of humans for nearly a century – except, of course, for the artificial water hole they use each day. The horses are scattered over 40 000 hectares of the Namib-Naukluft National Park. How they came to exist here as the world's only desert-living wild horses is still anybody's guess. But, as with most mysteries, there is much speculation.

Where did these marvellous mounts come from? The University of Kentucky says they're mostly Shagya Arabians from Hungary – crossbred by German colonial forces in South West.

To explore one of the possible origins put forward, you have to drive more than 150 kilometres northeast to Duwisib Castle, which was built by Hans-Heinrich von Wolf in 1908. An aristocrat and artillery officer and someone who adored a raucous party, Baron von Wolf and his American-born wife Jayta bought

Above: Small clumps of wild horses trooping in for their morning drink.

Previous page: A solitary wild horse finds slim pickings in Namibia's southern desert lands.

the property and built a *Schloss* (castle) on it. And when you travel through Namibia, you'll soon get used to these *Schlösser* popping up from time to time. But *Schloss* Duwisib is still one of the most remarkable.

More than 20 oxwagons packed to the rims with furniture, building material and fancy goods came from Lüderitz in the west. Master stonemasons and carpenters arrived from Europe, wells were successfully discovered and sunk and a massive forge was built, which produced everything from horseshoes to the ornate wrought-iron latticework for the castle's windows.

Just before the beginning of the First World War, Baron von Wolf started a horse-breeding station at *Schloss* Duwisib. He doted on his horses, spending

an inordinate amount of time and attention on their stabling. But in 1916, after he had left Duwisib and was killed in action at the Battle of the Somme, what happened to his horses was never recorded. Could these be their descendants?

Jules later spoke to Telané Greyling, a young woman doing her doctorate on a management plan for the horses through a South African university.

'I think it's highly unlikely that the horses would have wandered this far south from Duwisib,' she said. 'I'm almost certain they came from a combination of German *Schutztruppe* and South African cavalry.'

When the area became part of the Namib-Naukluft National Park in 1986, a solar-powered pump was installed at the water by the government. Underground water was pumped up for the horses, and a hide was added so that their drinking sessions could become tourists' photo opportunities.

In summer, when the plains grass is abundant, the horses' survival seems effortless. But in winter they move slowly and their heads are always downcast, searching for *Eragrostis* grass. Sometimes they seem to be nibbling at nothing but gravel, and their energy levels are at a dangerous low.

These horses have been through several drought-induced genetic bottlenecks. Over the years, the horse numbers have fluctuated dramatically – as low as 60 and as high as 300 at times, when the rains have been good. In 1992, they were suffering so badly from hunger that the Ministry of Environment and Tourism sold off 100 horses to eager buyers all over the subcontinent. It supplied the remaining 80 with fodder. Telané Greyling and a friend bought 15 of them and brought them back to a riding school in South Africa.

'We found they have a very passive disposition,' Telané said. 'That's part of their survival strategy.

They have learnt not to stress. If a domestic horse was dehydrated the way these horses are on a regular basis, it would die within two days – of stress, not dehydration. But the desert horses have adapted to being dehydrated regularly and to having sparse food. They're philosophical – they accept their conditions.'

The horses have also adapted to the heat. During the middle of the day, when temperatures can easily rise to above 40° Celsius, the horses turn their backs to the sun so that it only shines down the middle of their spines.

The horses' harsh world means that only the very fittest survive. Foal mortality is high – in some areas as high as 90 per cent – because the horses often have to move 40 kilometres between grazing and water, and their stallion pushes them mercilessly. A foal with the slightest weakness or defect will become hyaena food sooner rather than later.

The horses have become so distinctive that experts have discovered a singular variation of blood type.

Called the Q Factor, it is found in no other horse on earth – a kind of mutation.

Telané has noticed that while the groups are small one family might, mostly at the instigation of the mares, join another group. But this does not mean that the two groups simply merge into a single entity; the two stallions totally ignore each other and service only their own mares.

'The bachelor males can be loners, or pair up with one or two others,' she said. 'Then there are the bachelors I call the Outsiders. Sometimes a bachelor will persistently hang around a group so long that the stallion tires of chasing him, and he's grudgingly accepted into the group. But he's never as charismatic as the stallion is and the mares don't often take up with him.'

Piet Swiegers, a long-time neighbour at Klein Aus Vista, begged us to tell the world 'not to go offroad, looking for them'.

'They're wild horses – treat them with respect...'
– Chris

Opposite page: The famous wild horses of Namibia, viewed from the visitors' hide at Garub watering point.

This page – Left: The horses move slowly to conserve precious energy in this bleak landscape. **Above:** Power pylons marching off like spindly techno-soldiers into the vast Namib. **Right:** The entrance to the colourful Baron von Wolf's Duwisib Castle – the disputed origin of some of the Namib's wild horse herds.

NAMIBRAND

Wind Tracks

DANCE OF THE WOLF

I'M DRIVING THIS BLOOD-RED SOFT-SHELL COROLLA INTO 'KHYBER COUNTRY', WHICH IN MY WORLD TRANSLATES INTO JAGGED MOUNTAINSCAPES, MOONLIT DUNES AND ROCKY ROADS. IT'S THE KIND OF PLACE WHERE YOU NOT ONLY GET IN TOUCH WITH YOUR INNER LIZARD, YOU ALSO YANK IT OUT AND FRENCH-KISS IT. YES, YOU'VE GUESSED RIGHT. I'M OUT HERE IN NAMIBIA AND I'VE BEEN IN THE SUN TOO LONG. AND THERE'S THIS LITTLE MATTER OF A FLAT TYRE.

Six hours from Windhoek's city limits, I arrive at the Wolwedans gate in the NamibRand Reserve. After a long, careful drive on the middelmannetjie road I see the farmhouse shining like a jewel in the late afternoon sun. I take out the wounded tyre and leave it beside the vehicle in the hope that someone from Maintenance can save it.

Now I'm escorted by Wolwedans's 4x4 to the main camp. The late sun turns a normally dull dune into something remarkable and the tufts of oryx-tail grass wave like amber fingers in the wind. Hermann Cloete, the manager, arrives for a drink at the canvas-enclosed bar in a room full of elegant desert-detail such as ostrich eggs and clay vases full of dry grass.

My chalet is the latest in *haute canvasse*: corrugated-iron roof, copper piping in the shower, wooden floors, a large veranda with benches and chairs, roll-down walls and the kind of eternal dune-view outside you'll be hearing about again and again.

What's also great is there's a rule about not walking out in front of the chalets, so guests can have total privacy. They can wander about their lodgings naked if the need arises. And there are no dangerous animals against which to roll the canvas down. The most nightmarish animal sound you will hear is the tap-tapping of little gerbil toes on the wooden porch outside.

Supper is cream of tomato soup, medallions of springbok, creamed aubergines, red cabbage and broccoli. And *malva* pudding (a hot baked dessert). And red wine, lots of it. And the exquisite singing of Frieda Kaiko, Lazarus Blaauw and Jacobus Swartbooi, who start their repertoire with a haunting hymn called *'/Gore'* (Give Thanks). They follow that with *'Koa pi re /iib a !Kai xuige'* (Worship Him Because He's Good). A week later, I'm wandering about my garden in Jo'burg and these tunes are drifting in and out of my head.

The stars above us look like a galactic jewellery convention (with De Beers as the prime exhibitor) and a sage person tells me that the Bushman name for the Milky Way is Backbone of the Sky. I return to my tent and it's very cold and just before I pass out I fancy I can hear gerbils morris dancing on the patio outside. Obviously, they're stamping their little feet to keep out the freeze.

Morning at Wolwedans is a trip. You drop down the front flaps and tawny eternity stretches out

Above: Into the mystic grasslands of southern Namibia ...
Previous page: Shape-shifting winds and afternoon light bring magic to the NamibRand.

before you. I marvel at this for a while, pull on something warm and venture out to earn my living with the camera. Within minutes I am dunestruck and photographing God's tiniest creations in the sand, without realising I've crossed into the front-of-chalet no-man's-land. I am almost instantly rebuked by Hermann Cloete, who's busy shaving. And quite rightly so. He has the interests of his paying guests at heart. I shuffle off to a safe spot, feeling mortified. Naughty, naughty me.

'Sorry I disturbed your privacy' is my mantra to all the guests at breakfast, and most of them seem fine with that ...

The NamibRand Nature Reserve is a conservancy of 13 farms and it backs onto the Namib-Naukluft, home of the world-famous Sossusvlei. After the Second World War, Jannie Smuts sold farms in this district to a number of his veterans at a nominal price. They introduced the hardy karakul sheep to these parts and the fur trade sustained them for decades. When fur became a four-letter word, the karakul business obviously failed. Which led to this

marvellous conservancy. I know I often said bad things about the bunny-huggers of this world in my foolhardy youth, but right here I have to fall on my knees and thank the lot of them. The NamibRand's most beautiful state is that of sandy wilderness.

The various farms that make up the NamibRand have wonderful names: Die Duine, Stellarine, Jagkop, Kwessiegat, Vreemdelingspoort, Draaihoek, Toskaan, and our very own Wolwedans. Now here in southern Africa, you'll often come across Afrikaans references to wolves: Wolweput, Wolwefontein, Wolwehoek, Wolwedraai and so on. Which is strange, because we don't really have wolves running about the place naturally. Only maybe on the huge spread near Philippolis, where Chinese tigers have been introduced – so why not wolves as well? Or kangaroos, for that matter? What about a small Tasmanian Devil?

The answer to all this is that the Boere were actually talking about hyaenas, of which we have plenty. Another thing they have in abundance out here is sunlight, so it makes good sense to use solar power at Wolwedans. Each chalet has its own panels. Even the waste water is utilised – the pipes run out onto flourishing *Acacia karroo* or *galpinii* trees. All tins and glass are taken to Windhoek for recycling and there are septic tanks, over which the tsamma melons grow discernibly greener. All firewood comes from Windhoek – they don't even pick up the deadfall out here.

My guide for the day is Canaan Ncube and his Land Rover is called Stretch. Canaan is a bright young Zimbabwean who used to be one of the Vic Falls river guides. If you know anything about Africa, you'll know that these Zambezi water rats attain the status of rock stars up there, so there's nothing wrong with Canaan's confidence quotient.

We drive off to Dune Camp to pick up some Swiss folk, wealthy and well-equipped people who spend six weeks touring Namibia every year. They can't get enough of the Big Sky-ness of Namibia and when they return to Chocolate Box Land they spend a lot of time wistfully poring over their thousands of African photographs. If I had an ounce of criminal blood in me, I would mug them for their superb photographic equipment, but that's another story.

Canaan Ncube tells us all about the camel-thorn trees, the dung beetles, the harvester ants and the oryx. But it's when we start discussing the fairy circles that my ears really prick up. You'll be driving through waves of blonde grass and suddenly come across a perfectly round empty patch. Go onto a hill, look down and you'll see thousands of them in every direction. Weird stuff. You mean to tell me, Mulder, that you actually think aliens landed here in their little battalions? Well, Scully, what other explanation could there be for this outrageous phenomenon? I don't know. Why don't we ask The Smoking Man?

Those pragmatists with no magic in their souls or salt in their snap beans say fairy circles are caused by termites and their enzymes. Here at Wolwedans, you can adopt a fairy circle for R300 and the money will go towards a trust to study these things further.

The drive through these remarkable plains is punctuated by lunch at a massive cluster of stones called The Hard Rock Café. The ever-present wind is howling like a banshee and whipping slices of cheese off our sarmies, the Swiss couple don't want to sell me their cameras, there is sand on my chicken leg and we ask Canaan why all the guides in this area go by biblical names like Isaiah, Obediah, Lazarus and, well, Canaan.

'People with names from the Bible have good luck in the desert,' he says cryptically and dusts off his chicken breast. All right then. Canaan is one of the best guides I've ever had. Maybe, also, the luckiest. – Chris

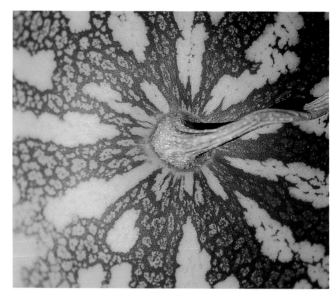

The Tsamma melon, with a high water- and protein content, gives life to both man and animal alike in the dry spaces of Namibia.

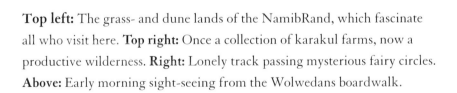

Top left: The grass- and dune lands of the NamibRand, which fascinate all who visit here. **Top right:** Once a collection of karakul farms, now a productive wilderness. **Right:** Lonely track passing mysterious fairy circles. **Above:** Early morning sight-seeing from the Wolwedans boardwalk.

SOSSUSVLEI

Sand Garden

Mystic Land

WE'RE HOT AND TIRED BY THE TIME WE ARRIVE AT SESRIEM AND THE SOSSUSVLEI LODGE. WE'VE BEEN RIDING THE ROCKY ROADS FOR ABOUT EIGHT HOURS. RICKY THE OBLIGING PORTER BRINGS THE KIND OF TROLLEY MOST SUITED TO LOADING TRAINS THE LENGTH OF AN OXWAGON.

Our luggage is grey with dust (as is our vehicle). I have a quick shower while Chris walks around taking pictures. Then I fall fast asleep, only to be woken by the staccato yips of the barking geckos at dusk.

The late afternoon in the desert puts back into you everything that the day took out.

The lodge, with its half-tent, half-building chalets, is amazingly comfortable. There is a notice informing you, the guest, of what to do in event of a sandstorm (shut everything you can, and if it gets too bad, retire to the dressing room, which is of brick).

We hold the Sossusvlei District Gin Rummy Championships in the tent and I win, but by a narrow margin. A gibbous moon rises over the Lodge tower. Springbok come down to the water hole to drink, moving about like ghosts.

We're gone before first light.

The gate to Sesriem and Sossusvlei opens at six a.m. and by ten minutes to, there is a small line of cars: Germans in front (in a hired white Mercedes) and a busful of excited Italians behind us.

While I get the permits at the office, Chris buys us the breakfast of champions: two mint ice creams.

In the distance, a hot-air balloon is rising above the jagged black mountains and floating towards the towering red dunes.

The tar road is excruciatingly bad. A sign every few kilometres warns you to stay on it, but the word *road* is no more than a euphemism for a potholed, ugly, tyre-wrenching experience.

Anyone who didn't know would think there are convoys of tipsy drivers around, because cars weave wildly along the road in a desperate bid to avoid potholes. Many have succumbed to the temptation of the much smoother gravel next to the road, but, like good citizens, we persist.

And here we are in the wind's Zen garden again. A plume of ostrich grass on a wind-combed red dune. A sinuous, sensuous curve of a star dune, the slipface lit red, the other side in shadow. The crests are invariably red, but the lower parts are often a fine cream colour, sometimes with dark lines that streak the dunes – signs of heavy minerals like ilmenite.

All along the road, people pull over to take pictures, unable to resist the contrasts of trees, grass and dunes. Each dune seems to have its own character and personality.

There are favourite spots for photography, and there are small gridlocks of tourists getting the ultimate shot. One dead tree framing a dune is a favourite.

At Dune 45, a group of cheerful, babbling Italians is climbing the mighty dune. Those who have toiled up

Above: Sossusvlei Lodge – a desert oasis built in a distinctive half-brick half-Bedouin style.
Previous page: Tourists at play on a Sossusvlei sand dune.

and giant-strided down the slipface are happily sitting on the protruding roots of ancient camel-thorn trees, shaking the sand out of their shoes. One is carefully filling a bottle with the dune's red sand.

The colour of the sand, with its rusting (oxidising) ferric-oxide incrustations in the sand grains, is a source of amazement to all. Later on, at Dead Vlei, we overhear a group of British tourists talking about the film made at Dead Vlei, starring J. Lo. They exclaimed that they thought the colours had been changed, that they were too surreal.

There are far more tourists, as well as buses and overlanding trucks, than there were the last time we were here.

We park at the 2x4 parking place and catch a Nam$80-per-person return ticket on the 4x4 ferry (Hobas Shuttle and Tours) taking people the five kilometres in heavy sand. Even at midmorning, we pass people trudging through the heat, with no headgear or visible water supplies.

We are with a German photographic group on the way in. They carry the most astounding equipment: heavy, long lenses, huge bodies. Keen as mustard.

We pass 'Big Daddy', or Crazy Dune, reckoned to be the highest in the Namib, and so one of the highest in the world, about 388 metres. And there, like a line of ants, a crazy group of tourists is moving steadily up its crest.

Dead Vlei is a 1.1-kilometre walk, following poles for markers across the rising and falling soft sand, from where they drop you. But it is worth every step.

The cream floor of the pan, the stylised dead trees, and the brown-red sand that surrounds it on three sides are astounding.

Above the vlei, people climb the highest dune, and then slide down the slipface, whooping. This is the world's largest sandpit for adults.

We also trudge to Sossusvlei and eat our well-earned breakfast bars in the shade of a sheltering camel-thorn tree, the sparrows chirruping beguilingly at us for crumbs. They are so confiding that they hop about under Chris's raised boot. They are followed by a hopeful tit-babbler and a passing tractrac chat.

We weave back along the atrocious road to pack up our goods at Sossusvlei Lodge and head north towards Solitaire.

At Solitaire we pick up supplies (Bovril, cheese, chocolate) and reacquaint ourselves with the tiny outpost. A country lodge has been built here since we last visited. And Percy Cross McGregor (a.k.a. Moose) is in a much better frame of mind.

According to local legend he has been the manager at Solitaire 'for as long as anyone can remember and is practically part of the furniture'. He's the source of unmissable home-made apple crumble and the daily fresh bread.

The last time we were here he was in a foul mood because a dreadful east wind had blown up a sandstorm and filled his general-dealer shop with a bus-load of entirely silent Germans eating their packed lunch in his shop, hardly buying anything from him except the odd slice of strudel.

Today he's cheerful and expansive. Business is clearly good and steady. I say we'd last seen him in a foul mood and he laughs.

'Sometimes the tourists just get on my nerves,' he smiles.

Someone once caught Moose in talkative mode and asked him why he'd settled out here, so far from things. He said he liked the barking geckos and the stars.

'It's like Nature switches on a Christmas tree here every night,' he said. Moose also made mention of 'The Bathing Ghost of Solitaire' who splashed around in his house at night and the Japanese tourist who had decided to walk 200 kilometres to the next town.

Previously we'd met a British couple in the middle of a windstorm at the Sesriem filling station. He was a frail, bespectacled 80-year-old (he nearly took off in the vicious updraft on his way to the gents) and she maternal, cooing and ten years younger. They were on a road trip through Namibia, driving in a decidedly nonmacho, soft-shell, Japanese vehicle around the country as if on an afternoon jaunt through the moors of Merrie England. We bumped into them later on a game drive in the north and he said: 'Yemm, good trip. Stayed over in Schwartzburg and had a fine time looking for the Southern Scrop. Great country, Nibia...'

I finally worked out he wasn't really gibbous, he was just describing Swakopmund, the Southern Cross and Namibia through dusty false teeth. It didn't diminish my deep respect for this octogenarian who was madly and happily overlanding in a big wild country with his wife and a roadmap full of strange-sounding names. A muscle car doesn't make you a real adventurer. Hitting the road with National Health choppers does.

On that same trip we discovered the joys of the cuddle puddle on our porch at Sossusvlei Wilderness Camp. It was full moon (just in case you were asking) and the gravel plains down below were sporting magnificent hair extensions of lemon-coloured bushman grass.

That day, we'd been chased up a black stony hill by a vicious yet rather doe-eyed ostrich. Breathless, we finally made it back to the lodge and recounted our near-death experience to the girl at the front desk.

'Oh, that would be Christine,' she laughed. 'Christine gets lonely for human company sometimes. She's totally harmless. A bit of scratching on the back of her head would have turned her all wobbly.'

Christine, we discovered, could do no wrong. A rich Italian female guest had recently demanded a cooked ostrich egg for her birthday dinner. Only Christine was around, and no male in sight. And yet, wonder of wonders, she went out back to the car park and obligingly laid an egg behind one of the game-drive vehicles. This incredible feat not only won her permanent mention in the Namib Book of Crazy Stuff, she was also voted Employee of the Month.

– Julie

Left: The arid air of the Namib Naukluft turns dead trees into art forms. **Below:** The grassy plateau below Wilderness Safaris' Sossusvlei lodge, where Christine the friendly ostrich roams.

Opposite page – Left and top: Two views of Sossusvlei at grassroots-level. Bottom: Nature's abstract art.

This page – Above: An early morning balloon ride. Above right: Wind-sculpted landscapes of Sossusvlei. Right: Sand-walking for the fit and keen.

And here we are in the wind's Zen garden again. A plume of ostrich grass on a wind-combed red dune. A sinuous, sensuous curve of a star dune, the slipface lit red, the other side in shadow.

Above the vlei, people climb the highest dune, and then slide down, whooping. This is the world's largest sandpit for adults.

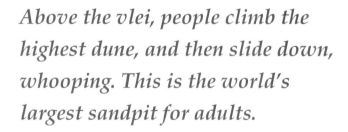

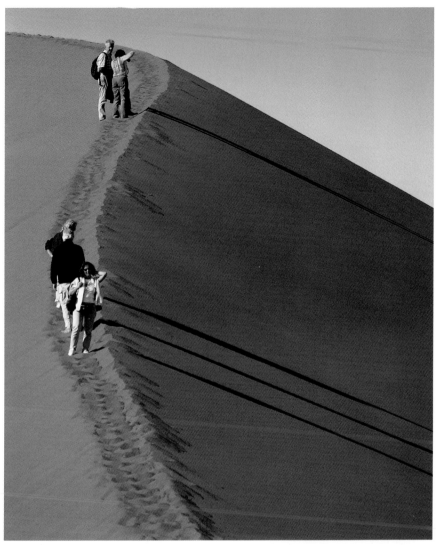

Opposite page: The Dead Vlei, with its stark treescapes, fascinates thousands of tourists each season.

This page – Left: Tourists cannot resist climbing the dunes, even in the heat of the day. **Bottom left:** Lizard life in the dunes. **Below:** A giant dune can begin with one grass tussock, some wind and a lot of sand.

NAMIB-NAUKLUFT

Rocky Ridges

CONCERT FOR DASSIES

IT'S HAPPY HOUR FOR SMALL WILDLIFE AT THE NAMIB NAUKLUFT LODGE WATER HOLE AND WE STALK OUT WITH CAMERAS TO JOIN THEM. THERE ARE GROUND SQUIRRELS, MOUNTAIN CHATS AND STARLINGS, AND THREE LARGE AS-YET-UNIDENTIFIED BIRDS FLY OVERHEAD AND LAND TEN METRES AWAY, GURKING LIKE BULLFROGS. WE ADVANCE SLOWLY, HALTING AT THE PERIMETER OF THEIR COMFORT ZONE.

To our bemusement they promenade calmly towards us, then stop at a grassless knoll to give us a rendition of a Rüppell's korhaan's full-throated, froggish croaks. After they've been to the rocky water point, they stroll up to us with an expectant look in their beady eyes.

Later we discover we've met August, Sophie and their daughter Petronella, who never left home. They are korhaans habituated to human company. If you keep very very still, they will take bread from your hand.

That night in the boma we feast on the best meat in the country – goat chops, boerewors, pork spare ribs and kudu steaks.

In a happy carnivorous daze we wander back to our room sated, and sleep like stones.

In the morning, before first light, we drive out to a little track off the C19, park and go for the most delicious two-hour walk. Chris stops and sings Neil Young's 'Helpless' in a canyon to invisible dassies opposite an old, dry waterfall. The acoustics are incredible. The whole valley rings with his voice.

Down the stony canyon, we pass *Commiphora saxicola* (related to Arabian myrrh – the balm of Gilead – or in Afrikaans, the *Kanniedood*) trees, rocks whitened over centuries by the viscous piss of dassies, portly phantom trees (*Moringa ovalifolia*), rocky hills with granite domes, sparrow-weaver nests, zebra-hoof tracks on the narrow paths, old bones in dry riverbeds, white-trunked and thickly leaved shepherd's trees, views over the petrified red dunes to the east. Millions of years ago, these dunes held still long enough to turn to red sandstone, still frozen in the shape of breaking waves, or so it seems from a distance.

Every now and then we come across a smell of cheap perfume – the flowers of a plant they refer to locally as the *Ngquni* bush, we find out later.

The Commiphora trees with their peeling golden bark light up against the rising sun as if they have haloes.

That afternoon we have coffee and *Kuchen* (cake) while manager Chris Baas (he says he has terrible trouble getting officials to believe this is really his surname) constructs a warthog *potjie* (iron-pot stew). The secret is never to use warthog fat, which is as rancid and inedible as zebra or horse fat, says Chris. He casually mentions a fact that affects my cold-meat consumption for the rest of my trip: salami is always made from horsemeat.

He's from the Damaraland area, and loves it dearly. They work two months on, one month off, and that

Above: A stately patrol of gemsbok in the dusk.

Previous page: A brace of Rüppell's korhaans in full song.

month he does not head for the bright city lights, but for a place where there are even more lights above, in the skies of the northern desert. Damaraland is where his soul calls home.

He used to be a guide until three years ago, but he tired of the endless road.

As we drink coffee, Chris gets up every now and then, dressed in a chef's apron that is huge, to add bits and pieces. This is not a traditional South African *potjie*, although that's the kind he prefers, the one that is cooked in layers. The Germans don't like everything all in one pot, so he does them separately.

First to go in is bacon, then the warthog, water and carrot, then greenery, such as dill and parsley, and a few vegetables, such as marrows.

As we leave Chris is wielding an enormous wooden spoon and looking like a cannibal chief as he shows the chef, Lebeus Shimonga (an Ovambo from Oshakati), the finer points of *potjie* making.

The other manager, Deon van den Berg, takes us out in the afternoon. We see at least 30 lively gemsbok in excellent condition. Behind them, turning mauve and grey in the afternoon light, are the Naukluft Mountains we explored this morning. The gemsbok's scimitar horns turn this way and that as they walk and graze. It looks like a medieval tournament, spears and sabres held aloft by carefree knights between jousts. Their stallion leader walks away from them, his head held low and nodding.

'He's not happy about something,' remarks Deon.

Deon is from the mining town of Tsumeb and was a mechanic before becoming a guide to Sossusvlei and then a manager there. He says he loves the Lodge, and the desert, and the way things change every day.

'Are you married?' we ask Deon.

'Nah, but I've got a bakkie and a horse,' he says.

He takes us up to their normal spot for sundowners, Marble Mountain. It is a long ridge, broken in three places, of pure white and pale pink marble. On top of the ridge, where the marble has been eroded into breeze-block-sized rectangles, the west wind sculpts it into fluted shapes. This is where the lodge's fine water comes from – the lodge bottles it too, under the label of Marble Mountain. The landscape looks parched and dry, but the water has never failed yet.

The other sundowner spot is harder to get to, on a long, smooth, granite ridge that requires 4x4 low range. They call it Honeymoon Mountain, because a doctor from Windhoek once (successfully) proposed to his girlfriend there.

The full moon rises like a silver coin over the pink-brown Naukluft Mountains. On the other side, the sun sets, leaving only a line of cloud lit bright orange. A camel-thorn tree clings to life on the crest of the hill, apparently growing straight out of the rock.

We toast the moonrise with Tafel beer, and drive back in the dark, seeing the odd springbok, pale in the moonlight, trotting with that no-nonsense head-down gait of theirs.

There is a famous Japanese model in the camp, and a crew of photographer, guide and driver, but we never see them. They leave before first light and return late. Apparently they are draping the Japanese model all over the dunes. Naked on the dunes in this heat? No one will say. – Julie

Left: Abundant birdlife in the trees in front of the Namib-Naukluft Lodge. **Below:** The brooding Namib Naukluft Mountains stretching up the coastline.

Left: Ground squirrel sentry takes his post in the Namib-Naukluft.
Above: Namib-Naukluft Lodge, nestled into a rocky hillside.
Right: The starting point of the two-hour hike through a world of dassies, canyons, dry waterfalls and Kanniedood trees.

SWAKOPMUND AND BEYOND

Old Style

SAFARI TOWN

SOME YEARS BACK A FRIEND AND I MET JAN VAN WYK AT THE SWAKOPMUND HOTEL. HE MUST HAVE THOUGHT WE WERE FANCY FELLOWS, BECAUSE OUR HOTEL WAS SWANKY AND OUR WHISKY WAS OF FINE QUALITY. SO JAN, OUR TOUR GUIDE FOR THE WEEK, WENT HOME AND PACKED THE GOOD CUTLERY IN HIS LAND ROVER.

He also packed two tents, a bread-making contraption, more red wine than a gouty toe can stand, starched linen, a table, chairs, and sleeping bags with special 'desert coverings' on them. Looking back on that time, I'm surprised he didn't throw in a brace of silver chandeliers as well. He had long, lavish breakfasts in mind, followed by an hour or two of driving and then an equally stylish luncheon under a thorn tree. Followed by another hour or two of driving and then a drawn-out dinner with gin and tonic and African anecdotes – which, let's face it, was the Rhino Tours Full-Nine-Yards package.

Instead, Jan van Wyk found himself with two guys – photographer Les Bush and me – who had fallen in love with the images of Namibia, two travellers who were more interested in getting dawn shots and word-pictures of this great land than in sleeping in and munching their way around the country. At first, we drove him a little batty. And then he fell in with our ways and ended up fully enjoying it.

Day one took us north and then east, as we swung off the coastal road towards the Messum Crater. It's formed like two overlapping concentric circles, 22 kilometres in diameter. Scrub desert, flatness and intense heat. Amidst all this grow the *Welwitschia mirabilis* plants. Some of them are 2 000 years old

and they looked like mourning widows with swaybacks. Ugly, yet venerable.

Prehistoric craters. Plants that were here before Europe's Dark Ages. Members of the human race are not counted as essential items in this place.

The first evening brought us to the Brandberg, a stand-alone mountain in the middle of the desert. We'd been told about Brandberg evenings, when the setting sun lights up the mountain in many hues of red. And up there, on its flanks and summit, the Brandberg has its own ecosystem that sets it apart from the intense, dry harshness below. Forests, springs and attendant life forms all flourish on the Brandberg.

'They even built an airstrip on top of the mountain,' said Jan. 'But the winds up there are quite rough. One day a pilot in a light plane flipped right over, crashed and broke both his legs. He still managed to crawl down the mountain and get help.'

Namibia, clearly, is not a country for wimps.

Jan wanted us on the other side of the mountain by five p.m., so he could set up camp properly, with bells, whistles and maybe some fresh-baked bread to go with dinner. But this was where we needed to be, for Les Bush to photograph the sunset on the Brandberg. The scheduled campsite was an hour's drive away. So we asked him please to find us another, closer

Above: Ancient lord of the Messum Crater: the *Welwitschia mirabilis*.
Previous page: Central Swakopmund could pass for a classic German Town.

place to bed down for the night. Jan said he'd try. I saw him scratch his head and look far out towards the darkening horizon.

With the Brandberg on film, we drove off and found a perfectly suitable spot on the lee side of a lesser-known hill. We drank a beer, wolfed down something quick and hot, jumped into our sleeping bags and were snoring away before eight p.m. With a bemused Jan van Wyk sitting solitary by the fire, sipping away at his merlot.

By four a.m. Bush and I were both awake, with eyes like racoons'. Around us, Namibia's nightworld chattered away like an insane chorus. The valley below was awash with silver from the full moon. In the distance, a jackal went trotting past in search of an insomniac rabbit.

Under Namibian skies, you get to see the stars of both the northern and southern hemispheres. The Southern Cross stands out clearly, ever a beacon to night travellers, such as the camel caravans of old. The Great Bear, *Ursa Major*, is another feature of the northern skies you can also see clearly from here. Caught between the endless lines of the Namibian

nightscape and its infinite canopy of stars, I was lulled back into a dreamless near-coma until dawn.

Most towns around the world are asleep on Sunday mornings. The town of Uis was seriously asleep. Just outside the settlement is a row of 28 graves. No plaques or headstones. Just plain grave markings in a line.

'Many years ago, a group of travellers going from Windhoek to Ruacana stopped to have a braai a few miles into the desert,' said Jan. 'They gathered wood from a euphorbia tree for the braai and made the fire. They tossed a sheep on the coals. The poison saturated the meat. Within hours, they were all dead.

'The Bushmen called the euphorbia juice "wolf's milk",' said Jan. 'They used it as poison for the tips of their arrows.'

No one had the key for the town's only petrol pump, so we had to wing it to our next destination, three sets of wary eyes on the gas gauge. We were headed for Okaukuejo, central Etosha.

On the way, Jan made photo stops for us at Burnt Mountain, where 120 million years ago a large mass of volcanic magma erupted through the earth's crust and lay burning for a long time. Now it's a big, brilliantly hued hill with atmosphere.

Not more so, however, than the Organ Pipes nearby. These are perpendicular slabs of basalt, a mere ten million years older than Burnt Mountain. Walking through this valley, you feel like Luke Skywalker on his approach run into the bowels of Darth Vader's Death Star.

At Twyfelfontein (see also pages 144–147) we were casually cursing the position of the sun, because Bushman paintings are not easy to photograph in the middle of the day. We were chatting away to our young guide at this site, who told us his life's ambition was to move to Johannesburg and be part of the jobless throng. And then Jan called us loudly from his Land Rover. The elephants!

'Namib Desert elephants,' he said, as we arrived, breathless. 'I've just seen at least five of them down at the riverbed.'

What followed was a slightly frantic rush in the vehicle to track them, and finally we were rewarded by the sight of desert elephants loping off at a surprisingly high speed. But they made far better midday shots than the rock paintings we'd just left.

By nightfall, we were in Okaukuejo Camp in the park. It was comfortable and we were still sleeping out under Namibian skies, but we were feeling slightly miffed because we had to share our space with other humans. The night before had been better, with just the three of us alone out there with our no-name hill and the full-moon valley below us.

Tourists gathered at the water hole for dusk shots of drinking elephants and horn-wrestling springbok. Oh well, we probably needed the shower anyway. But the urge to get back out there and taste the life of a desert wanderer was very strong.

Touring Namibia is like venturing forth through a timeless, unlimited, natural cathedral. Finding little relics and places of worship, spotting wild animals, marvelling at the bird life and all the crazy formations of rock that come at you constantly. This is one of Africa's Disneylands. The Mystic Land. You find The Mystic in the second bend of the Khyber Pass, the blackness of an orang-utan's eyes in Sarawak, the swing of a Patagonian gaucho's whip, the stance of a Mongolian wind-wrestler, and out here, on the outrageously blonde plains of Namibia. The Mystic is an Eric Clapton outburst on a Fender Stratocaster, fine red wine, a beautiful woman with a sense of humour and timing, and evensong in an Anglican country chapel. The Mystic is what we all live for – that sense of deep magic that lies all around us, in wait.

The next morning, we drove north to Opuwo, Namibia's version of *Mad Max*'s Bartertown. Or perhaps the intergalactic bar scene in *Star Wars*. This is a melting pot of dark looks, tribal Ovahimba maidens sitting in ochred splendour in the shade of the bottle store, Portuguese traders, mystery men with perhaps some *klippies* (illicit diamonds) in their pockets, sweaty tourists in huge overland Unimogs – a rough and ready settlement where, if you're clever, you'll juice up and move on.

Outside Opuwo, Jan took us to an authentic Ovahimba village and within minutes our new best friend was busy treating a child's horrible hand-burn – the baby had fallen into the porridge pot days before and the wound had festered.

Presently, we found ourselves driving through a tortuous pass on the way to Sesfontein and a hot spring called Warmquelle. A bad driver could have had us flaming out a thousand times along the way, but Jan patiently coaxed the Land Rover through this stony hell.

That night, we slept next to one of the world's most naturally soothing, blissed-out places. Again, we were history by eight p.m.

The dreamtime came along. Friends from all stages of my life came to visit and to talk. I awoke at four a.m. and lit a smoke, watching slinking shadows in the riverbed, listening to big fat frogs romancing each other, the moon hanging like a ripe grape in the ink-sky.

'This wasn't always just a warm-spring place,' muttered Bush, rising from sleep. He was right. Warmquelle must have been an ancient church of sorts in the days before the 4x4s. The local inhabitants must have worshipped the cool, clear, sweet water – the most precious commodity in a bone-dry country – if nothing else.

Most days, we drove in silence around this vast country, looking out at the land and its changing forms. We were now back at the coast, and the atmosphere had chilled right down. Jan told us about the mist and how it supports an entire ecosystem that never sees real rain: beetles, lizards, lichen and snakes that gather up the minute particles of water and use every atom of liquid in the air.

Flocks of seagulls flew across the grey dunes from the sea, mussels clasped firmly in their beaks. Hovering briefly about six metres above the road, they dropped their cargo on the hard surface in the hope that the mussel shells would crack open on impact.

Then they swooped down to devour the contents.

'And they tell me birds are dumb,' said Jan.

The Skeleton Coast is littered with the rusted wrecks of ships and with bones belonging to all manner of sea life. It's also stark and lonely, and the roar of the Atlantic only adds to the eerie silence of the coastline. This is where you can see the brown hyaena, its fur matted with salt water, patrolling the beachline for carrion and the occasional ghost crab scuttling about.

We had to photograph a shipwreck. For such an image, we had foregone the overnight pleasures of an in-country rest camp with all the amenities. We found our wreck, photographed it fully and then camped at Mile 108 outside the Skeleton Coast Park.

The wind was blowing like blazes, so we pitched camp against a toilet facility. Jan could not understand us: get up before dawn, have no breakfast, drive like hell through the heat of the day, miss lunch and then spend sunset working. And now this. Were we deliberately looking for hardship and suffering? We laid our stretchers out and invited him to put his bedroll in between ours.

'Not a damn,' he said. 'You guys wake up in the middle of the night and chatter like bloody mon-keys. I'd rather sleep up here, on top of the Landy.' Fair enough.

We then proceeded to sleep for a full 12 hours, burrowed deep into our sleeping bags, with heavy canvas rolls covering us against the raging winds and flying sand.

Last stop on the trip down back to Swakopmund was Cape Cross, where the seals hang out in their thousands. Watching them en masse was like viewing an animal TV sitcom: they bark at each other, they argue, they make up, they gossip, they weave about and generally behave like the Married with Children cast.

After a week of living rough with Jan, we returned to Swakopmund with stubble on our faces and wonder in our eyes. Somewhere along the line, we had been touched by The Mystic of Namibia.   – Chris

This page – Below and bottom: The massive, barking seal colony at
Cape Cross. **Right:** Zebra and springbok gather at Etosha's Okaukuejo
watering hole.

Opposite page – Top left: Termite high rise development in the Kaokoveld.
Top right: Messum Crater on a misty morning. **Bottom left:** Lichen detail in
the Messum Crater. **Bottom right:** The salt road between Swakopmund and
Cape Cross.

RETURN TO SWAKOPMUND

On the Strand

Love in the Laundrette

AFTER NEARLY THREE WEEKS OF MOSTLY GRAVEL TRAVEL, ALL NUTS AND BOLTS ARE SUSPECT AND DUST HAS CREPT IN EVERYWHERE. THE CAMERAS ARE MAKING DUST-SPOT PICTURES AND RATTLING ON THEIR MOORINGS. IT'S TIME TO VISIT FOTO BEHRENS IN SWAKOPMUND FOR A SERVICE.

The owner, Henning, is a tall man in a leather waistcoat that he wears like a second skin – sensible for this unpredictable Swakop weather. He has seen this problem many times, because tourists keep drifting in like woebegone waifs, bearing sick camera equipment.

Cheerfully, Henning tightens the Sony's little nuts and makes it all better, then poofs a little air into the innards of the Canon and advises specialist attention and 'some Adobe for the spots when you get home'.

But there's more. He has advice on conditions up north, where to buy the special shells and tobacco the Himbas love and how to find the Moon Landscape outside town. Henning is so friendly and *gemütlich* (warm) that we hardly notice spending more than a grand on blank CDs, lens filters and a miracle cleaning pen. It's worth every Namibian dollar. Henning, we feel, has saved our bacon...

Later we get a permit to visit the moonscape. Driving out, I think we were already in it. If it weren't for the power lines, it would be like a completely different desert, featureless once you've crossed the Swakop River with its green reeds and standing water.

There is nothing except the odd small, dark, dry bush clotting the sand here and there. All of a sudden, though, the flat ochre sand breaks up into millions of little hillocks, strange undulations – the moonscape.

Driving back, we're just in time to see the sun dip below the horizon next to The Tug, staring out to sea. I mention to Chris I've never seen the alleged green flash that happens at sunset, and, as I say it, the sun vanishes, leaving, for a brief emerald moment, a green flash. I whoop and people stare.

In the morning, mist cocoons the town, wrapping it in pale grey. Difficult photo conditions. While Chris takes pics, I have my shaggy-dog hair cut at a salon near the restaurant.

The Damara and Ovambo women here speak fluent German, Afrikaans and English, and live in the township we'll be visiting in the afternoon: Mondesa.

'When the tourists come past we always wave to them,' says the lady who shampoos my hair.

They quiz me about Johannesburg: 'Are there rich people there? Poor people? Is there a factory nearby? Are South Africans Christians?'

They tell me many white South Africans are moving to Swakopmund, with holiday homes along Long Beach.

Chris, in the meantime, has found us some kudu veldskoen, a comfortable shoe that needs no socks, a speciality of Swakop. There are also sealskin shoes, but we refuse them.

Above: Swakopmund – springboard for adventures.
Previous page: Swakopmund's beachfront promenade, where everyone goes in the summer season.

The day is spent mostly trying to take pictures in light that comes and goes. But mostly goes. The museum has the new addition of a People of Namibia display, which is excellent.

The next day we head off early to Walvis Bay to get the engine seen to at Pupkewitz Delta. It's been sounding a little wheezy. Unsurprisingly, the air filter has to be replaced after all that dust-road travelling. More than 5 000 kilometres on the clock.

We have toasted sandwiches at Rootman's Home Industries and watch the locals come in and buy *vetkoek* (a fried cake made from unsweetened dough) and coffee for breakfast.

We drive to the waterfront and are entranced at the sight of dozens of greater flamingos foraging in the shallows. Chris has his eyes on the pink birds

as he descends a rocky bank, but, alas, the last half metre is slick with oil and he lands on his bum with startling rapidity, fingers cut and bleeding.

The bloody flamingos have politely walked away from the scene of the accident, leaving us little to photograph anyway, after all that.

Later, we take a walk around Swakop, hoping for a bit of sun. It is as if we are in a bell jar of mist that completely flattens and depersonalises the light.

We visit the Kristal Gallery with its massive quartz crystals, the biggest in the world, and escape into a world of strange names, colours and formations, minerals forced into beauty by unimaginable heat and pressure, chalcedony, sulphur crystals, pietersite (only found in Namibia and China, and named after the Namibian guy who discovered them), jasper, tiger's eye, tourmaline, garnet, amethyst.

As we get out, the lid of mist over Swakop pops off and light streams into the town. We walk about, shooting pictures of churches and beautiful buildings.

We also pass the Bargain Corner, which advertises poop scoops and furniture inside. I have to explore. While Chris has a smoke outside, and with two shop assistants gawping, I make a list of what I find on the jumbled shelves: crystals, calculators, Venetian wineglasses, wooden carvings, warthog-tusk bottle openers, second-hand crockery, old copies of Jehovah's Witness *Watchtower*s, gaslamps, dolls (Herero and Himba), second-hand meat-mincers, calabashes, teaspoons with crests from all over the world, watering cans, mediocre paintings, second-hand books in German, new furniture, old bottles.

Back at the Hotel Schweizerhaus, we are pursued up the stairs by the sweet nutty fragrance of the *Strudel mit Sahne* (thin, filled, baked dough with cream), Black Forest cake, almond pastries and freshly ground coffee of the Café Anton.

Our balcony gives us an ever-changing view of tourists haggling over animal carvings with vendors in the street below. Bits of conversation from the coffee shop below drift up to us in American, South African, German and Namibian accents. The dusky sunbirds weave between the flowers and above it all, at balcony height, a small colony of escaped budgies in shades of bright green and electric blue are making a very happy home among the palm trees and araucaria.

From our balcony we can also see the top of the red-and-white lighthouse, which flashes its signature pattern to passing ships from dusk till dawn.

Through the trees, we glimpse a statue to the *Schutztruppe* who fell in the Herero War.

Just after lunch, I have a cup of coffee with hotel and Café Anton owner Heidi Snyman in her office while Chris gets up close and personal with a Black Forest cake.

Heidi was only five when her parents opened the hotel and Café Anton. She and her sister took over from them in the early 1990s and all the recipes follow the family tradition.

That night, we tackle our enormous bag of laundry and take it to Joy World Laundromat.

Here in Joy World, they've turned a dismal laundry chore into a great big night out, with video games, a bar, snooker tables, vending machines and a huge notice board announcing fêtes, special trips, discount adventures and such. The people in here are locals, hotel workers and backpacking tourists.

Outside in the mist, at the back of the brewery, the Betty Boop sign announcing the pleasures of Joy World stands out proudly. The security guard is also a laundry expert and shows us how to work all the machines, even comes around from time to time to check on the progress of our T-shirts, socks and undies. It's amazing what gets shoved to the bottom of your travel bags after three weeks in-country. Some of the socks are starting to develop minds of their own, trading partners and wandering off across the room like woolly zombies in search of a night out.

While the rest of Swakop's upmarket tourism sector is sitting down to a seafood platter with some good Cape wine, we're cheerfully reading penny-horrible, trash novels in Joy World and chewing on breakfast bars.

That night, in an idle moment, I start reading verses out of Revelations aloud to Chris from the ever-present Gideon Bible (there are usually two to a double room). Chris warns me that frightening your travel partner with tracts from the Gideon Bible constitutes the first warning of insanity on the road.

– Julie

Semi-precious stone display at the Kristal Museum, Swakopmund.

Above: One of the oldest hotels in Swakopmund. **Above right:** Detail at the local casino-hotel. **Left:** The sweet-tooth section of Café Anton. **Right:** Craft stalls near the beachfront.

We are pursued up the stairs by the sweet nutty fragrance of the Strudel mit Sahne, Black Forest cake, almond pastries and freshly ground coffee.

This page – Above left: The breakwater guards the Swakopmund beachfront. **Above:** Swakopmund's seafront splendour. **Far left:** Swakopmund is one of Namibia's best loved playgrounds. **Left:** The Strand Hotel along the Esplanade.

Opposite page – Top left: Namibia makes some of the world's best beer. **Bottom left:** European architecture lives on in this African desert town. **Top right:** A Cape vulture keeps a beady eye on visitors to the Swakopmund Museum. **Bottom right:** Remains of a desert elephant and other Namibian creatures at the Swakopmund Museum.

The lid of mist over Swakop pops off and light streams into the town.

MONDESA TOWNSHIP

Outside Swakopmund

LIVING IN SAND

IN HIS BLUE MINIBUS, TOUR GUIDE BEETLE GERTZE DROVE US OUT TO MONDESA TOWNSHIP — THE 'BACKSTAGE' AREA OF SWAKOPMUND SO FEW TOURISTS EVER SEE.

Beetle, a local plumber out of tourist season, gave us a quick historical rundown on his neighbourhood: 'Mondesa was created in the 1960s by the South African apartheid government, who moved all the black people out of town. They also separated the different tribes within the township, and gave them different privileges. The Damara, with generally paler skin than the blacks, had the biggest houses. Then came the Hereros, who must have won the South African government's respect for the way they stood up to the German colonialists. At the bottom of the pile were the Ovambos.'

Ironically, the Ovambos are the majority-tribe of modern-day Namibia.

The front yards of the houses were swept clean, and their porches displayed pot plants and various flea-market adornments. There was very little litter about. Most of the homes were painted pink, yellow, purple and blue.

It is customary for all the residents of the township to put up a white flag outside a house where a soon-to-be-married person lives. They leave it fluttering there long after the wedding – until there is nothing left of it. If there is a death in the family, a black flag with a white cross will be displayed outside the house – and removed after two weeks.

Beetle took us to meet an extraordinary Herero woman called Naftaline Mauha, who wore a voluminous, leopard-print bustle and a traditional 'horns of the cow' headdress. We had first seen these unusually formal outfits in the Botswanan frontier town of Maun, gateway to the Okavango Delta. You'd expect desert-dwellers to wear something lighter.

'Well,' smiled Naftaline, 'we didn't always wear these outfits. We used to dress like this.' And she pointed at a little doll, skimpily dressed in ochred animal skins.

'The Himba,' I said.

'The Hereros and the Himba, we are one and the same,' said Naftaline. 'When we lived in the country, it was fine to dress in skins. But there were always problems back in the old colonial days, when we came to town. So we began dressing like the missionaries' wives, with eight layers of skirts, and they approved.'

The Herero people, according to Naftaline, wanted to preserve something of their own culture. Their cattle were central to their lives, so they devised a cowhorn-shaped headdress. The women, in their generous dresses, were also encouraged to walk slowly when in public.

'With the grace of a cow,' said Naftaline.

Naftaline's people came from across the Kunene River in Angola, migrating south in search of better grazing. In the Kaokoveld, some stayed and are known today as Ovahimba. The rest of the Herero nation moved into central Namibia and down as far as the Swakop River.

Although she dressed like a missionary's wife from a century earlier, Naftaline was deeply involved in current issues. Working as an AIDS counsellor, she travelled around the township giving home-based care to the sick and supplying clothing to struggling families and bandages to those with open wounds.

This sprawling settlement in the dunes was the 'reception area' where people applied for formal housing and then waited their turn. Pit latrines, 'smart' cards for water and a five-dollar taxi ride to town – a hard life out in the desert. The only supplied electricity came via streetlights, and a soup kitchen came out on Saturdays.

We stopped over at the house of Ernst and Elsie Taniseb. Ernst was an 'opportunist artist', the only breed of creative person that could really survive out here in a world of sand, wind and dramatically reduced circumstances. We wandered around his amazingly higgledy-piggledy dwelling, full of found objects and initiative.

'Seventy per cent of this house is recycled materials,' he said, lurching a little to the left.

'Where does it all come from?' I asked.

'From the DRC Hardware Store,' Ernst laughed, with a touch of bitterness. 'That's the local rub-bish dump.'

Plants were happily growing away in old tyres. The fence and walls of the house were made from scraps of wood, with the occasional strong plank for support. There was an old generator under cover.

'Whenever I've collected enough money for a bit of petrol, we run the generator and watch some television,' he said. Ernst painted T-shirts and sold crystals for a living. But he was probably the most environmentally successful man we'd met in Namibia so far, and his pride and joy was the 'grey water' flush toilet he'd recently built for the women in the family.

Above: Naftaline Mauha, Herero woman in leopard-print, lives outside Swakopmund.

Previous page: Ernst Taniseb plays some Damara blues outside his house in DRC Section, Mondesa Township.

The Taniseb house sported images of Jesus, reggae stars Lucky Dube and Bob Marley, and a glazed-eyed trophy of a red hartebeest that Ernst had found out at the 'hardware store'. While he took his battered old guitar out and began playing as the mist rolled in over the DRC, I went out to where Elsie and her mother, Francisca, were sewing a duvet cover. Granny Francisca was a fine-boned lady behind large spectacles, and I asked her which language she preferred me to address her in, English or Afrikaans.

'Mevrou (madam in Afrikaans), I am an Afrikaner,' she proudly announced, and continued sewing. Who said Afrikaans is dead? There's a whole bunch of Damara-Namas out there in the wilds of Namibia who would disagree wholeheartedly.

Our next stop was at the home of Stanley Witbooi, descendant of one of Namibia's greatest leaders. Stanley was born with 'the caul' and, in the Nama tradition, was raised to be a healer. He took out bottle after bottle of seeds, pieces of bark, roots and even seal oil. He also took out an old brass cigarette lighter, which worked with flint and dried grass.

'This belonged to Hendrik,' he said. Stanley told us about Nama 'bush tucker', traditional medicines and how sticking to the 'old culture' gives you long life.

'We had a Nama woman around here who died recently, at the age of 126,' he said. 'She would still be alive if only she hadn't smoked so much.'

We returned to Back of the Moon where, over a couple of Tafel lagers, Beetle narrowly beat Chris in a friendly game of pool while someone played a CD of Angolan love songs and our little fan club of kids gathered meekly at the threshold of the bar. Then we all washed our hands and sat down for an Ovambo-style supper. We ate millet pancakes, wild spinach, soft beans and the finest, crispiest mopane worms this side of the Limpopo River. It was a good day to remember.

– Julie

Above: The young face of Mondesa Township, a many-layered settlement outside Swakopmund. **Right:** Life in the desert – marginal in Mondesa.

Left: Children gather for the camera in Mondesa's main street. **Above:** Entrepreneurship in Mondesa. **Right:** One of the township's hairdressers. **Below:** The crude fire station that serves the township residents outside Swakopmund.

CAPE CROSS

Jackal Coast

SEALS AND LICHENS

THE NAMIBIANS CAN BE A TAD SPARING WITH THEIR ROAD SIGNS. JUAN AT CAPE CROSS LODGE GAVE US THESE DIRECTIONS TO FIND THE MYSTERIOUS MESSUM CRATER: 'TURN NORTH AT THE LODGE GATES ONTO THE SALT ROAD. EXACTLY 1.7 KILOMETRES FROM THERE, YOU'LL SEE A FEW ROCKS ON THE SIDE. TURN RIGHT. YOU CAN'T MISS IT.'

Actually we could and we did, but no matter. We are used to being navigationally challenged. We finally went back, measured the distance to within the quarter metre, and turned right onto an unpromising dirt track next to a few small rocks, gasping as it swiftly expanded into an informal six-lane gravel highway out of sight of the main salt road.

We were on a welwitschia mission. The guidebooks to Namibia assured us that the most handsome specimens were to be found around the Messum Crater – a place receiving scant attention, even on detailed maps. Chris had seen a single, unspectacular example years before, and still nursed grave doubts about their innate loveliness. I had never seen a welwitschia in the flesh, so to speak.

So midmorning found us driving eastward, through milky weather, along a track that had mercifully narrowed. Finally, intrigued at why the dirt road seemed a consistently paler colour than everything else, we stopped to take a closer look, and then fell to our knees in wonder.

Before us, stretching endlessly to the dark gravel horizon, was a jewelled miniature wonderland of lichen, dozens of kinds. Some were bright orange or faded green, patterned in concentric circles. Others were like small lacy ferns. Some spread over pebbles like dark tea leaves, or rose up like petite forests. Then there were ones that were brownish and crustose, turning the earth strangely crystalline underneath.

The most spectacular, always mentioned in guide books as being rare and unique to Namibia, is *Teloschistes capensis*, a fluffy orange matting resembling Martian lawn – home to 17 mite species, I was happy to note. One becomes inordinately excited and reverential over the smallest signs of life in deserts.

Even more exciting was the *Teloschistes* sprouting happily in old tracks of vehicles. The Namibian Ministry of Environment and Tourism has been fighting a patchily successful battle for years against heedless drivers of 4x4s, whose tyres have destroyed entire lichen ecosystems and whose tracks have remained for decades. The lichens were reclaiming their land.

Welwitschia mission entirely forgotten, we pored over four square metres of small stones, exclaiming over tiny pieces of quartz or dolomite turned into miniature Fabergé eggs by the lichen.

The diffuse grey mist had kissed each lichen-enamelled stone with a light sheen of moisture and each one extended every possible surface area upwards to absorb it, glowing with vivid colour.

Above: Cape Cross, where seals used to be recruited for the circus in the Victorian era – or so the legend goes.
Previous page: Well-fed duo of black-backed jackals near the seal colony at Cape Cross.

I rocked back on my heels and wondered quietly how many species before us had not even been described. A book on the back seat of the bakkie, *Biological Diversity in Namibia*, revealed that while the country had an extraordinary number of lichen species, many found nowhere else, very little was known about them. 'Due to the uniqueness of the lichens, overseas specialists find identification difficult and time-consuming and the majority of species can still not even be identified to genus level,' wrote one of the authors, Patricia Craven.

It was an hour or more before we lifted our heads to the horizon again. And there, *mirabilis* of *mirabilis*, was a welwitschia in a nearby riverbed – the dry Messum River. Whooping in the muffled solitude of the mist-cloaked desert, we ran towards it like children on Christmas day.

The *Welwitschia mirabilis* lay unmoved, ruffled and unkempt, inscrutable and bafflingly unlike any other plant in the world. Charles Darwin once described the welwitschia as the platypus of the plant kingdom.

This one was a comparatively large specimen, a female, which had been a seedling maybe around the time the Greeks were getting snippy over Helen of Troy. The long trailing leaves, torn to ribbons by the wind, sheltered two kinds of strange red and yellow bugs – as it turned out, the welwitschia bugs, in nymph and adult form.

Mary Seely, in her book *The Namib: Natural History of an Ancient Desert*, notes that botanists are still bickering over how this ancient plant – specimens of which can live to thousands of years – should be classified. It is grouped with the pine trees, but has a few characteristics of the more advanced flowering plants, and one very primitive feature shared with the club mosses.

It is a law unto itself, found only in the inhospitable Namib desert, and is actually a tree – a desert-surviving minimalist with its two long, trailing, dishevelled leaves attached to two curved, boat-like, woody frames.

The riverbed was as dry as white bone. When last had it seen a torrent rushing down its sandy, sinewy length? But obviously there was still moisture deep below it, because there were many welwitschias, all apparently growing vigorously.

Further on into the crater, the welwitschias shrank in size, and then started petering out. Even the lichen vanished. Eventually there was just the distant rim of high hills on the horizon in all directions around a small conical hill, with everything in between filled with evenly spaced volcanic stones – the remains of a great volcanic upheaval millions of years ago.

But by now it was lunch time, and the considerable culinary gifts of Cape Cross Lodge chef Herman Awaseb were calling.

A short drive from the lodge is the enormous seal colony of Cape Cross and the *padrão* (stone pillar) erected by Portuguese navigator Diogo Cão in 1485, three years before his countryman Bartolomeu Dias sailed past this point, around the Cape and along the long-sought trade routes of the East. Even so, the almost forgotten Cão was the first European to sail 'beyond the barrier of fear' that lay beyond West Africa's Gold Coast.

On the original *padrão* (now replaced by a replica), Cão left behind a quaint inscription in Portuguese and Latin. The English translation reads: 'In the year 6885 of the creation of the earth and 1485 after the birth of Christ the most excellent and serene king Dom Joao II of Portugal ordered this land to be discovered and this padrão to be placed by Diogo Cão, gentleman of his house.'

The rocks and stone cross stand silent, but the seals do not. There are somewhere between 80 000 and 250 000 Cape Fur Seals here. The smell is daunting until you get used to it – fortunately the lodge remains free of niff – but the spectacle is hypnotic. Everywhere you look there are noisy seals. Seals sleeping, bickering, honking, squabbling and mock-biting, blinking soulfully, arching themselves in yoga positions, feeding bawling babies, hauling out, hauling in, bellowing, or blissfully scratching themselves with their silly hind-flippers. There is every shade of sealcoat, from the fat black pups, fading to chocolate, through dassie brown, olive-grey and pale coppery Weimaraner.

In *On Wings of Fire*, legendary travel writer Lawrence G. Green interviews one August Hasselund, employed at the sealing station in the 1930s. He not only clubbed them for a living, but was also a bit of a seal wrangler. He told Green: 'Eh vurk mit der yong seals – tich dem dricks for der circus.'

It appears that the seals of Cape Cross were, according to Green's sources, highly prized for their intelligence and poise – and made especially fine circus animals. They were, said Hasselund, even better than California sea lions in this regard, although the latter had been taught to say 'I want my mama' on certain notable occasions. And this was something no Cape Cross seal had been able to muster thus far.

According to Hasselund, a good circus seal should possess thick whiskers with a downward curve – and its nose should not be pointed. Where would it then be expected to balance that rubber ball?

Seals with the dropsy or short attention spans would not do. They were known as snoozers, and weeded out soon enough. No one likes a narcoleptic performer in a circus. You needed barkers. They were the winners. Always on the go, ready to dart about at the slightest command, eyes bright and whiskers trembling.

'Eh loff der seals an' der seals loff me,' Hasselund declared to Lawrence Green.

Mr Green made a literary meal of this frontier spot in Namibia, and loved to take photographs of the seals of Cape Cross. In *So Few Are Free*, he advised: 'There is only one way, I found, to photograph the seals at close quarters. I had to set my camera, race towards the colony so that they could not pick up the scent, leap over the rocks and take my picture without a second's delay. They all came sliding past me in a panic-stricken cavalcade. This method, however, is not without danger. A large bull weighs up to eight hundred pounds, and some will attack and maul a man. They will grip a man's arm, worry him like a terrier with a rat, roll on him and crush him. They know what they are doing on the rocks, those seals, while a man can find no foothold. Men killed by seals have a little cemetery of their own on the shore at Cape Cross.'

Well, that other great travel writer, T. V. Bulpin, says there is no record of the Cape Cross seals having attacked human beings. So we contacted the good folk at Cape Cross Lodge later and asked them to check for us. There was indeed a cemetery, but it carried no evidence of seal-on-human violence. Another of those Namibian mysteries.

Some latter-day advice for seal-snappers: take a long lens, stay behind the wall, focus in on the action and have a good time. There's no need to test the power of a bull seal's teeth on your arm, or his terrier-like tendencies.

On the fringes of the colony lope opportunistic black-backed jackals. En route to the lodge we stopped to admire a young female gazing about her with a self-satisfied air as the wind ruffled her foxy black-and-silver cape.

That evening, we drank chilled white wine in the cosy bar with owners Adri and Gustav Holz, discussing the extraordinary luck that had enabled them to establish this luxurious lodge on the last bit of privately owned beachfront land north of Henties Bay.

We were leaving early the next morning. 'But you haven't been to the Brandberg and the Bushman paintings yet,' protested Adri. 'Or the shipwreck on the Skeleton Coast. Or the tour of the salt factory just outside, where they export organic salt from the pan all over the world. Or Torra Bay, to some of the best fishing in the world.' Next time.   – Julie

LIKING LICHEN

- In the Namibian desert, lichens are considered extremely important. They stabilise desert sands, increase soil nitrogen, are often the first species to colonise naked rock and provide habitats for tiny insects and even food for antelope species. The Damara terns use lichens as shelter and nesting material. Yet lichens are easily destroyed by vehicles' tyres.

- Lichens are one of nature's puzzles. They grow in the most environmentally hostile places, in severe cold, heat and drought, but they are vulnerable to air pollution. They are beautiful and useful, but cannot be cultivated. They live on rocks, yet sometimes eat away their own foothold.

- Centuries ago, even educated people thought that lichens were stones caught in the process of becoming plants.

- Botanists are fond of saying that lichen provides the only equation where $1+1 = 1$. Each single lichen is made up of a fungal partner and an algal partner. The algae provide energy from photosynthesis and the fungus provides structural and reproductive benefits.

- The perfume industry is probably the greatest user of lichens – about 9 000 tons of two types of lichen are picked every year in the former Yugoslavia, France and Morocco, and a kind of oil, which acts as an odour fixative, is produced from them.

- Lichens easily absorb particles from the air, making them extremely sensitive to air pollution from the burning of fossil fuels – specifically sulphuric oxides.

- The greatest potential use for lichens is still being studied. Some species have been used to treat rheumatism and arthritis. Others produce a kind of antibiotic that may be useful to humans. In certain lichens, scientists have recently found compounds that seem to inhibit reproduction of the human immunodeficiency virus (HIV).

This page: The macroscopic world of lichen in the Messum Crater, complete with a Welwitschia beetle that goes bustling through it.

Above: Cape Cross Lodge – sophistication on the Skeleton Coast. **Right:** Decades-old tracks of 4x4s in the lichen fields. **Bottom:** The close-up magic of lichen.

Centuries ago, even educated people thought that lichens were stones caught in the process of becoming plants.

Above: *Welwitschia mirabilis* on the plains of the Messum Crater. **Top right:** Rock level at the Messum Crater. **Below:** A well-fed coastal jackal. **Right:** The Cape Cross padrão.

Top left: A gull on the lookout for scraps. **Top right:** The 'old man' of the Messum Crater. **Left:** Seals in doze mode. **Above:** A spider at home under its lichen rock.

SKELETON COAST

Shipwreck Shore

ROARING BEACHES

WE ARE ONCE AGAIN ON THE SALT ROAD, HEADING NORTH INTO THE SKELETON COAST PARK. THE GATES AT THE OFFICE ARE ADORNED WITH A MASSIVE SKULL AND CROSSBONES. PIRATES AND SHIPWRECKS AND MIST AWAIT US.

As we head north, we catch a BBC Radio news report about a dreadful hostage crisis in Russia. Soon it fades into static, and we are pleased to leave the fraught world of current affairs behind us. The music of Mr Van Morrison suits our purposes better.

Our first stop after the gate and crossing the Ugab River is a wreck. Much to our delight, we have the place all to ourselves. The wind-scarred sign reads 'SL Seal 1976' – that's all we can make out. The weathered wooden frame still remains, and the rusting iron of the winch. There are a few fishing nets. We stalk the shipwreck like cats with our cameras, Chris giving me lessons all the way – get a situation shot, don't get footprints next to it until you've finished with those, get textures of the wood …

The next attraction is the Huab River lagoon, with its white-breasted cormorants lining up for photographs along the turquoise coloured water. There is also a lone young greater flamingo, its wings only pale pink still, not scarlet, which paces away as Chris pursues it with his camera. Finally, it leaps into the sky and flies away.

Close by is an old oil rig, collapsed into the sand. Its gantry, now lying on its side, is being used by white-breasted cormorants as a breeding platform. Who was drilling for oil here?

It looks like a dreamscape where the world of humans is returned to the world of nature.

At the turnoff to Springbokwater, the landscape settles down into rocks, road and distant sea.

After Torra Bay (a settlement of toilets and not much else), we start wondering what on earth Terrace Bay is going to be like. The landscape turns otherworldly on us. There is nothing but garnet-coloured gravel, rocks and creamy sand showing through every now and then, like the belly of a beast.

It feels as if we are the last people on earth. What could there possibly be at the end of this long, long road? Our itinerary promises breakfast and dinner. We wonder, in mild giggling hysteria, whether we might *be* them.

This must be the most remote place we have ever been, the most remote place on the subcontinent. It feels like we're headed for the resort at the edge of the world.

A weathered skull-and-crossbones sign welcomes us to Terrace Bay. Large machines are standing on the right. A mine? And then a settlement of beige prefab buildings. This is it. We walk into the prefab office to check in, interrupting a game of pool.

A man called Daniel checks us in, gives us Room 12. I flip through the visitor's book, and read a few rave reviews about the home-cooked food and a heart-warming confession by a man from Nelspruit talking about a long-promised trip with his dad all the way from the south of Namibia to here, how his dad taught him to fish using redbait and sardines and how, although they didn't catch anything, they had a wonderful time.

The whole camp is empty except for the room right next to ours.

This is clearly a place for men doing a bit of bonding over fish and alcohol.

At supper time we go up and have a few Tafels at the bar, and watch the highlights of the ODI (one-day international) between England and India (India got caned) with the staff before going through and having an unidentifiable but inoffensive kind of soup, meat for Chris, fish for me (came with a side order of mussels) and a strange salad of grated carrot, pineapple and many olives. Tinned fruit and custard for dessert.

The real delight is the pebble beach, with millions of extraordinarily beautiful, smooth-rolled stones. The stone collector in me starts to go a little crazy, and when we return, both my hands are full. Green, white, red, blue stones. Forget the fish. To me this is the real attraction, this and the clucking sound the waves make rolling the stones around.

Amongst the pebbles, which come in all shapes, patterns and sizes, are the regular Skeleton Coast found objects: crab shells, seaweed, bits of rope, driftwood and, if you're lucky, some ship tackle that's washed in. All along this stupendously bleak and lovely coastline are bits of boat, wrecks and overboard objects. Each, again, with its own little tale to tell.

I also remember the posse of pied crows in the children's dilapidated playground beneath the restaurant, my mood suddenly matching the dull-grey

Above: Beware, ye litterers of Henties Bay – a mock gallows at the entrance to the town.
Previous page: Weathered remains of a ship that came to grief along the Skeleton Coast.

Atlantic horizon to the west. My husband, however, has a very different reaction to Terrace Bay. – Julie

The mist rolls in from the sea, as Sir Paul McCartney would warble, and we're here, at the veritable end of the world. As we know it. The last time I felt so secluded in a place was on the island of Jura in the Inner Hebrides of Scotland, where George Orwell sat down and penned 1984 in utter solitude. Terrace Bay is good for fishermen, remittance men, outlaws from suburban TV and writers wanting a bit of space. Not always good for photographers, although, when the mist rises, the dunes behind us are spectacular and the pebble beach is a treat.

The waves rattle the stones and wash them and caress them and massage them and ruffle them and then retreat, causing the pebbles to shiver in an anxious drumroll of departure anxiety. I haven't seen gulls here, only pied crows hanging about the children's playground with its broken fishing skiff and tatty hobbyhorses like conspiratorial gangsters planning a dustbin heist.

I think of our first night here, being served by a waiter wearing a nightwatchman's greatcoat and offering, albeit kindly, a choice of 'de fish, de meat' – and, to start, 'de broda' – bread wrapped in cellophane to keep it from drying out and going crook.

I could come up here to write something grand, although chances are I'd look deep into a bottle of Old Brown and come out tatty the other end. It's bleak, with its deserted diamond-mine gear and skeleton entrance sign, worn by wind and looking like something out of a horror movie, but it's also very beautiful in that same way. Like a really good-looking woman with a broken nose. In this lost world up here, north of most things bright and sunny in southern Africa, you feel cast away from that world you drove out of. Even the road to Terrace Bay is like an avenue of very little you're familiar with – 'moonscape' springs to mind.

Compare this place to the other Atlantic spots of Namibia: bright new Lüderitz, cheerful Swakop, suburban Henties Bay. It just lurks up here and promises you prefab huts and top-class angling. And for many two-boy teams of city runaways in 4x4 bakkies, that's about all you really need out of a weekend.

In short, I like Terrace Bay. It's skanky, it's real. And if I ever learnt to fish, I'd come here for my first lessons.

– Chris

Nature strikes back – what was once an oil rig has now become a breeding ground for white-breasted cormorants.

Above: Rock garden at Henties Bay.
Above right: Forbidding landscape up the Skeleton Coast. **Right:** Welcome to Terrace Bay – the fading pirate sign says it all.

SERRA CAFEMA

Krokodilla

THE LAST RESORT

DROPPING INTO THE REMOTE HARTMANN'S VALLEY IN A LITTLE CESSNA WAS VERY CLOSE TO MY IDEA OF A MOON LANDING. THE VASTNESS OF SAND AND ROCK WAS BROKEN ONLY BY A WILDERNESS SAFARIS VEHICLE APPROACHING IN THE DISTANCE, DRIVEN BY GEORGE KATANGA OF SERRA CAFEMA CAMP. A PLACE VERY FAR FROM THE MALLS AND BOULEVARDS OF CIVILISATION. THE LAST RESORT, SO TO SPEAK.

Cafema was a Portuguese explorer over in Angola, and a range of mountains on that side was named after him. The wilderness camp lies on the Kunene River, not more than 60 kilometres east of the Skeleton Coast. George drove us through a little Sahara of sand blown up against dark granitic outcrops, tortured lizard-lands with mica schist glittering like space dust on the windblown dunes.

The final descent into the pass leading to the river was spectacular. First, there was a controlled plummet down a dune slope, then up a granite hill. At the top, shining silver in the sun, was the great, serpentine, green-fringed Kunene – a water-miracle in this steadfast, stoic desert.

'*Kunene* means "right arm" in Himba,' said George, 'the inference being that "right arm" is really big. *Kaoko*, on the other hand, means "left arm" or "small".'

Serra Cafema is one of the world's truly spectacular areas. Even after travelling so far through this visual giant of a country, it was still like coming from a land of little chapels into one awe-inspiring cathedral.

This great valley, which is split by the Kunene, was formed by glaciers about 280 million years ago, give or take a week or two, I suppose. This fact lies embedded in the *Atlas of Namibia*, which also gives the country's 'donkey density' as 140 000. Give or take.

'Crocodiles are the border guards between Namibia and Angola out here,' said George. Upon our arrival at the camp, co-manager Robyn Dreyer warned us not to:

• Succumb to the temptation of an unaccompanied midnight skinny dip in the river;
• Even walk within three metres of the water line;
• Trail our fingers in the Kunene while on the evening boat trip.

'The crocs will have you,' she assured us. 'They surge out of the water at more than 70 kilometres an hour. You won't even see them coming.'

The next morning our guide, Toni Hart, took us on a river walk. A grey heron lifted itself from the rocks and flew off, a graceful Japanese painting come to life. We spent a few precious moments with a drop-dead gorgeous Violet Dropwing dragonfly dressed in party colours and then found some African wildcat tracks heading under the kitchen.

'He lives there,' said Toni. Sensible fellow.

I got that Hollywood Apache feeling again, of being watched from above. And yes, there they were, a troop of baboons disappearing over a dune. They

Above: The Bogenfels range of rocks near the Kunene River.

Previous Page: Arguably the most famous Himba woman in her district, Krokodilla survived a Kunene croc attack.

left behind a scout to trail us and occasionally bark progress reports back at them, while they cavorted like olive circus clowns on the sandy ridges.

Some Himba donkeys spied on us through salt bushes.

'Trans-Kalahari Ferraris,' said Toni.

An African pied wagtail bobbed his tail at us from a *Salvadora* bush, and we met the common fiscal with its pronounced white eyebrow, a feature not seen anywhere else. We stopped at a silver-leafed saucer-berry bush and sucked on its yellow fruit, which was so sticky it clung to our teeth for dear life.

'The Himba cook them into quite potent liquor,' said Toni. Every species on God's earth, it seemed, has a way of getting out of it.

While we were temporarily lost in a world of white-winged *Tenebrionid* beetles, purple winding morning glories and baby-crocodile tracks, we were hailed from behind by a cheerful old man called Dos Santos, who was on his daily fishing mission.

Dos Santos carried a pole strung with an old fishing line, ending in a home-made hook with a wine cork for a float. We asked him – in Portuguese

pantomime – what he used for bait. He scrabbled about in a tatty old bag and brought out a tin half-full of soil and nervous worms.

Dos Santos, a sensible man of his time, had simply walked out of Angola and its wars in the 1970s and set up home alone in a tiny hut made from branches next to the Kunene River. He did odd jobs for the lodge and was growing butternuts, pumpkins, carrots and corn for its table.

Utterly fascinated by this happy old Huck Finn, Chris and I swerved off the scheduled walk and followed Dos Santos to his fishing spot, a nearby river backwater. Our baboon sentry barked: 'Two pax veering off with Delta Santa. Three pax still on path. Leave some lunch for me.' Or something.

We asked about the crocs. Dos Santos said they left him alone. We gave him some tobacco money and the old man put down his fishing pole, lifted his hands to the heavens and invoked a sky-full of blessings upon our heads. We blessed him back and rejoined the main party.

Presently we found ourselves on a rocky peninsula with a splendid view of the Kunene pouring itself enthusiastically over a waterfall. Above us in this watered garden moonscape, a black-chested snake-eagle circled. At our feet, a tiny orange-and-brown skink scurried, occasionally halting to lift its feet and cool the pads under them in a weird canoe-paddler imitation.

'A Mexican Wave lizard,' I said.

'You're getting the hang of it,' Toni said.

On the way back we looked in on Dos Santos, who was singing a cheerful song (a) because he had not yet been snaffled by a Kunene crocodiles, and (b) because he'd already caught a thicklipped happy (*Thoracochromis albolabris*), two leopard squeakers (*Synodontis leopardus*) and a slender stonebasher (*Hippopotomyris ansorgii*).

What's more, he was going to eat those fine specimens all by himself that night, outside his stick-hut along the Kunene river, by the light of an Angolan moon. What's not to sing about?

There used to be elephants here, browsing the length of the Kunene in great numbers, until the war wiped them out. On the evening boat trip, we wondered if the area would not be more generously lined with makalani palms had the soldiers and their machine guns and the grey-shoed politicians in the background spared the herds. Someone, I think it was Toni, had told us a makalani seed germinates more easily once it's been through the digestive tract of an elephant. All life is connected.

A hot, heavy, desert wind blew at our backs like the urgent breath of a panting dragon. It batted our boat towards a tiny sandbank, which was technically on the Angolan side of the river.

On the return trip, Toni waved farewell to an almost-invisible Dos Santos as he sat on the bank taking in the last glow of sunlight. There was something so essentially happy about that man, I just wanted to jump out of the boat and go and sit by his side. But

I knew the crocs would show an unhealthy interest in my plans.

The next day, we went for a drive out to the Bogenfels arrangement of rocks. We passed Ludwig's bustards patrolling the sands for crickets while the skies above built up into a stormlight fantasia.

Suddenly, Toni stopped the vehicle and dived into a sand dune. She was hunting down an armoured lizard that lived in the dune. The lizard was not in for visitors.

'He knows me too well,' said Toni, rejoining us, dusting off half a dune from her ranger outfit.

The images you find in Namibia's northwestern deserts often test the imagination. The various massifs take on the shapes of barking dogs, sharks and dragons. There's always the chance of spotting a shaggy brown hyaena trotting over the dunes.

In the afternoon Toni drove us off to meet Oumatjie and Krokodilla, who live in the village of Otapi about eight kilometres from the river. Four years ago, Krokodilla (who then bore a now-forgotten name) went off to the Kunene to fetch water, accompanied by her little dog. As she was filling her calabash, a crocodile leapt out of the water and grabbed the right side of her body. The dog charged the crocodile, barking. The distraction worked – for Krokodilla anyhow. The big lizard released the young Himba woman and went for the little dog, which was never seen again.

'Somehow, Krokodilla managed to drag herself ashore,' said Toni, who had befriended both women. 'She was flown to Windhoek for surgery and stitched up. She recovered well, and wore her hospital gown for many months afterwards. Krokodilla is well known among local Himbas for having flown in an aeroplane and having been to Windhoek. They sometimes mention the croc attack as well.'

We met the two rather gorgeous women in the late afternoon. They received us in their village. Oumatjie, a little tetchy but entranced with Toni's flame-red hair, was making a basket from makalani palm leaves. Krokodilla, about seven months pregnant with her fifth child, was enjoying a bit of pipe smoking. I don't know what she had in that pipe, but she looked more relaxed than a Cape Town lounge lizard. Which is hard to do.

We took our photographs, bought some PVC bracelets and said goodbye to this little family in the sand.

It was a brief, reasonably gracious encounter, with Toni being a good facilitator, talking in pidgin Himba.

After breakfast the next day, we prepared to leave. The dune baboons were out on the sand doing an interesting set of dervish-cartwheels as if they were on a four-day acid rave in the desert. The African wildcat under the kitchen had eaten the rather handsome lodge rooster in the night and the Brits were practising on their quad-bikes in the car park. The lodge at the end of the universe was dealing with another day in paradise.

– Julie

One of Namibia's many dry rivers seen from the air en route to the Kunene River.

Opposite page – Top left: Serra Cafema is surrounded by dramatic landscapes. **Top right:** Quad-biking through the scrub desert. **Bottom left:** The sparkling, life-giving Kunene River. **Bottom right:** Krokodilla at her homestead.

This page – Top left: A baboon lookout keeps a close watch. **Top right:** Dunes and rocks lining the Kunene. **Above:** A thick-toed gecko takes a break in the shadows. **Right:** Flower shadows at midday.

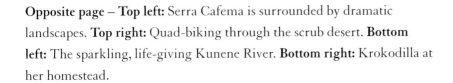

Right: A heron takes flight. **Below:** The delicate ecosystem of the northern desert plains. **Far right:** The sandy, sloping drive to the lodge.

Left: A lone Himba hut in the middle of precious little else. **Bottom left:** Tourists on their early morning adventures through the desert. **Below:** The donkey – favoured mode of transport along the Kunene.

KAOKOVELD

Village Life

BARTER TOWN

WE DROVE ON INTO AN ETERNITY OF MOPANE FORESTS TO FORT SESFONTEIN IN THE HOANIB VALLEY. THIS IS THE LEGENDARY PLACE OF THE 'SIX SPRINGS' THAT HAVE NURTURED LOCALS AND TRAVELLERS FOR CENTURIES. THIS IS WHERE THE COLONIAL GERMANS BUILT A FORT — JUST FOR A CHANGE.

Fort Sesfontein was abandoned by the time the First World War came around and has now been renovated into a very attractive lodge. We weren't staying on, but that didn't stop us from having a drink and a discussion with the helpful barman about animal husbandry.

The road from Sesfontein to Opuwo is a bit of a cultural strip mall. Herero and Himba hopped out from the shade to flag vehicles down. They wanted a lift, some cash or perhaps a T-shirt for barter. A long-limbed, athletically naked young Himba girl twirled around dangerously close to the road, her clay braids swaying and her braceletted arms beckoning for us to stop.

We were not going to fall into a Himba village, hand out breakfast bars and shoot pictures. We were going to pay for a proper, guided experience, so we continued into the Himba capital of Opuwo.

Now there's a frontier town for you, quite correctly called Opuwo, which means 'The End' in Ovahimba. Think of far-flung outposts, where cultures meet and mix and match; where cowrie shells work as well in trade as Namibian dollars; where out at the airstrip the bush pilots gather around the fuel depot and swop flying adventures; where two massive Damara bulls gather their forces in the swirl of a sudden dust storm and crash heavily into each other; where you

feel about as off-planet as you've ever felt before. I half-expected to see Jabba the Hutt come waltzing down the main road. Or the ghost of Humphrey Bogart over by a roadside bar.

We were booked into a tented camp outside town. It was set beside a dry riverbed and covered in sand.

'Welcome to the dirtiest, dustiest topless bar in the world,' said our host.

But hey, this was Opuwo. Take it all with a pinch of salt. Or sand. You can be what you like up here. And believe me, the longer you stay in Opuwo, the more you like it. We later spent a night in a lodge in the centre of town, surrounded by six thumping discos that hammered on until the early hours. But we didn't care. This was Opuwo, where they have a special way of doing things.

One afternoon we met Matirepo Tjiraso (Marty), a pleasant Himba man who would be our guide to a selected village. He drove us south through Opuwo in his minibus.

'This town gives me a headache,' he said. 'I love going home to the kraal. There, it's peaceful. I need nothing. If I need meat, I slaughter a goat. If I need milk, there are cows. In town, you need to pay money for everything, and you struggle to pay it. I watch the people in the streets of Opuwo, they just walk up and then they walk down again. In the country, there is always something that must be done.'

Marty warned us that we would probably not see Himba men in the village. The drought had forced them to take the village cattle deep into the mountains for grazing.

We arrived at a village called Oatotati, which means 'area with many small mopane' in Himba.

It was hairdressing time. Women sat in the shade working on each other's braids. The beauty of a Himba cultural experience, I thought, was that you see the Himba people in their natural state. They don't suddenly run behind a hut and drop their jeans and running shoes for loincloths just to please a tourist. In that way, they share a lot with the Maasai from Tanzania and Kenya.

The headman was in the hills. His wives were off at a funeral. So the village granny was in charge. She was a feisty soul, naked to the waist and covered in ochre.

'Morro,' we greeted the granny and the girls, as we had been instructed to do. We were introduced and allowed to photograph them.

We learnt about the Himba habits, their holy fire system, the naming of children, how many cattle have to be killed at a headman's funeral, how much a dowry amounts to, the significance of their jewellery, how they concoct the butterfat ochre for their bodies and the many medicinal uses of the mopane leaf. And then the girls started to ask us questions.

Were Jules and I married? Did we have children? Why not? Where did we come from? How many days would it take to walk there? Thank God I could hide behind my cameras, because some of those questions were tough.

A baby bawled from inside the kitchen area. The headman's niece sprang up like a gazelle and retrieved the small boy. She clamped him to her coppered breast and he subsided into contented silence.

Two pregnant women emerged from a hut and posed for us after putting on their special leather skirts. They were expecting babies 'when the rains come'. The statuesque woman who had been plaiting the headman's daughter's hair gathered up her baby in a beautiful kaross and walked across a clearing with him in graceful, light strides. In the distance, the senior wives were returning from the funeral in another village. We offered our gifts to one of them. She graciously accepted, peeping inside the packet and nodding with satisfaction before handing it to the granny. She wished us a safe trip. We wished them 'good rains'. Marty brought out a crate of mealie meal, sugar, coffee and tea. The visit was over.

That night, at a barbecue, we spent a few hours with Namibian guides Uwe Mueseler and his son Larrigan, from Tsumeb. The conversation shifted many ways, from weird Namibian-English (Namlish) to fiercely defended views on Land Rovers versus Toyotas, to best camping spots in the north. We then went back to our tent and slept under the curled tail of Scorpio and the Clouds of Magellan, just up the road from the Milky Way.   – Chris

Previous page: A Himba grandmother outside her village near Opuwo.

This page – **Above:** The Namibian landscape is often witness to pure, hard-core survival. **Right:** Two Himba matriarchs return to the village after a funeral in a neighbouring settlement.

Opposite page – Top: Weaver nests are often the only signs of life in the dry season trees. **Bottom left:** Baobabs begin in the Kaokoveld. **Bottom right:** Himba huts – practical and insulated against bad weather.

We learnt about the Himba habits, their holy fire system, the naming of children, how many cattle have to be killed at a headman's funeral, how much a dowry amounts to, the significance of their jewellery, how they concoct the butterfat ochre for their bodies and the many medicinal uses of the mopane leaf.

PALMWAG

Nelson the Camel

ROCK RHINOS

KAPOI KASAONA FROM WILDERNESS SAFARIS' RHINO CAMP IS A MODERN HIMBA WHOSE FATHER HAD BEEN DETERMINED TO EDUCATE HIM WELL. HE SPOKE TO US ABOUT HIS DAD, WHOM HE OBVIOUSLY ADMIRED GREATLY.

'My father says if a thing is not planned, it's not worth doing at all,' he said.

Kapoi had begun working locally for the Save the Rhino Trust some four years before, doing camel patrols to track the rhinos on this huge wilderness concession of half a million hectares next to the Skeleton Coast National Park.

'In the 1960s this used to be farm land,' he told us. 'Cattle, sheep and goats were here, but there were also about 300 black rhinos. Then the border wars began, and so did the poaching for rhino horn. The locals mostly did the shooting, the South Africans mostly did the buying.'

Soon, there were only about 30 rhinos left in the whole area. Then Blythe Loutit formed the Save the Rhino Trust.

Today, if you ask the environmentalists about numbers in the Palmwag area, they'll naturally be coy in answering.

'It's a very special animal,' said Kapoi. 'We're talking about *Diceros bicornis bicornis* – the desert-adapted black rhino.'

Wilderness Safaris and the Save the Rhino Trust had brought tourism to the area, and the community was seeing the benefits. Schools and clinics had been built, and locals were being trained as guides and trackers and lodge staff. Rhino Camp had become an international lodestone for students and scientists – a day spent in the gravel fields of this moonscape in search of wandering rhinos had become one of the country's top adventures.

'But,' said Kapoi, 'the best kind of rhino encounter is when the animal doesn't even know it's being followed, so there's minimal stress. The guides always try to bring the tourists in downwind of the rhino, so it never scents them.'

A black-chested snake-eagle banked over us in the late afternoon. The dense air of sea level and the softer light somehow conspired to make it enormous, like a condor. We drove past smelly shepherd's bushes with the basalt of the Etendeka Mountains jabbing the sky and then arrived at the clear pools of the Uniab River. Cresting a hillock, we came upon hundreds of springbok in a slowly moving tapestry of creams and fawns doing the *trekbok* thing, ambling to the horizon in search of something that might be nice to eat.

Just after a ruby sunset, we bounced into the camp, which was set in a lake of plumy lemon-tinged grass in the light of a grapefruit half-moon. There we met relief manager Andrea Staltmeier, bearing cold wet towels for dusty brows.

Wake-up was before first light. By 6.30 a.m. we were on our rhino-tracking expedition. By the cold light of dawn I had a prickly feeling at the back of my neck. I just knew we were being watched from somewhere.

Above: A black rhino challenging all who come near.

Previous Page: One of the anti-poaching patrol camels used in the Palmwag area.

And there they were, the canny beasts, lining the ridges of Damaraland. Looking down at us from a safe distance. Then wheeling in fresh sunlight and galloping off like the magnificent Hartmann's zebras we knew them to be.

We stopped beside an ant nest, which was ringed by a handy harvest of grass seeds.

'The Damara people collect these seeds,' Kapoi said. 'They soak them in water for three days and then add honey.'

There was silence.

'And then what?' I asked.

'Then they drink it. Very potent. Very delicious,' Kapoi added with a touch of mischief.

When you go tracking black rhinos out here, you actually spend most of the day with your nose in wild lavender, ostrich salad, medicinal Himba plants, fluffy ice bushes and the indomitably green mustard bush, the *Salvadora persica*. We tried the *Salvadora* berries, which both elephants and Himba delight in, and they tasted like a blend of English mustard and horseradish.

Another *Salvadora* tip: the fibrous stems are used locally as toothbrushes.

The basalt rocks began to take on weird shapes in the growing sunlight, and Chris, with his macro lens, found some form of life behind almost every stone. On one kopje the bleached branches of dead shrubs looked like the skeletons of a platoon of soldiers who died trying to the take heights.

The radio finally crackled.

'John, John, I'm standing by,' responded Kapoi in Afrikaans.

A little while later we came upon John Hendricks, a Damara from Sesfontein who had become a local tracking legend. With John were two trainee trackers. They were after two rhinos who had caught their scent earlier on in the day and had led them on merry 20-kilometre chase to an oasis on the Uniab River.

The trainees looked like they were seriously reconsidering their career choices. John, despite having slogged all day over stony ground, looked fresh and ready for another trek. We peered into the thick riverine bush.

'Hell of a place to lose a rhino,' someone whispered.

We retreated to high ground, the wind blowing steadily in our faces. A fog bank full of sullen clouds rose from the west, where the Uniab joins the Atlantic. The wind was driving in from the western ocean side, snaking into the desert along the riverbed.

We all decided to have lunch and rethink our strategy. Kapoi and co. whipped out tables, camping chairs and a repast of quiche, meat pies, salad and maize-meal bread with jam.

After lunch we followed John and saw the rhinos, a mother and a four-year-old calf, in a longish depression in the ground. Ma had tremendous dinosaur-like horns – a regular little fat triceratops. Grey, antediluvian lumps moving confidently through a brown stony desert.

We ran up a hill to get a vantage point, ducking to keep our silhouettes from breaking the horizon line. Ma had definitely sensed something down there. She swivelled and glared short-sightedly up at the top of the hill, her young boy taking cover behind her.

Mother and son stood posing for photographs, turned swiftly and jogged off into the horizon, tails curled pig-like over their backs.

The next morning, on our way back to the airfield, we were given an amazing *pronk*ing display by a resident herd of springbok – they were darting about, throwing themselves crescent-backed into the sky, like little jump-jets trying to escape their skins. Full of beans. The girls in the herd looked suitably impressed.

We came across a Namaqua sandgrouse sitting on her eggs in the folds of a welwitschia – a sight I'll probably never encounter again – then across a Rüppell's korhaan being mobbed by an angry gang of finchlarks. The korhaan was trying to gobble down a baby finchlark as fast as it could. One of the French tourists with us spotted a leopard at a riverbank. The rest of us missed it, but within minutes we were surrounded by curious Hartmann's zebras we'd surprised sunning themselves on a ridge.

Suddenly a tiny three-day-old oryx calf, fawn and startled, wobbled across the road into a thicket. Its mother had probably given instructions for the calf to lie still close to the road, but the vehicle noise made it totter up and stumble away. Further on, Kapoi pointed out a scrub hare, lying still as a stone under a bush, not even blinking. Becoming Damaraland.   – Julie

Opposite page: A Namaqua sandgrouse mother on her camouflaged nest within the sheltering arms of an ancient welwitschia.

This page – Above: Fearsome but harmless armoured ground crickets occur in great profusion at certain times of the year. **Right:** Hartmann's mountain zebras keep watch from the safety of ridges. **Below:** Tourists on the drive through the vast wilderness concession near Palmwag.

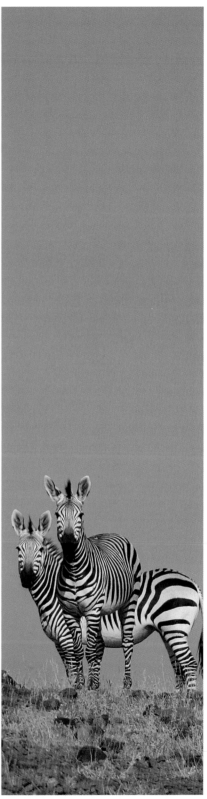

Top left: This is black rhino country. **Above:** The rough terrain around the Palmwag concession. **Left:** One of the Palmwag camels taking an evening stroll.

Above: A dead tree punctuates the harsh scenery of Damaraland. **Top right:** Palmwag Wilderness Camp – one of the top lodges in the area. **Right:** Three eggs in the well-camouflaged nest of a Namaqua sandgrouse.

KHORIXAS ROAD

Tyre-biter

A Day in Damaraland

IN THE BIG PICTURE OF AN OVERLAND TRIP AROUND THE VASTNESS OF NAMIBIA, THE LITTLE DRIVE FROM THE SKELETON COAST TO THE DAMARA CAPITAL OF KHORIXAS MIGHT SEEM LIKE A SPIT IN THE WIND. A MERE TRAVELLING BAGATELLE.

So that's what we're thinking one soapy mist-light morning at the Uniab River mouth while two flamingos wriggle their toes in the delta mud, scaring up all manner of crustacean for breakfast. It's going to be 200-odd kilometres of mostly OK gravel travel to the overnight stop at Khorixas and in our Ninja pick-up we'll probably make it by lunch time.

A chestnut-banded plover darts back and forth at the lapping water's edge and a Cape teal with its upturned pink bill paddles out past the shallow and ducks out of sight while Bob Dylan whines bravely from his album *Love and Theft* in the double-cab.

Just after the ghostly, swirling silence of Torra Bay (out of fishing season), we take the C39 inland, heading east. It's just Jules, me and Bobby and the barchan dunes with blue-grey rocks and washes of garnet sand on their flanks.

We come upon a range of rocky hills, reddish-grey below, pale-green on top. Time for a belly safari, because these outcrops are literally covered in lichen and we've got a macro lens itching to go to work. There is thick white lichen with black spots, concentric orange lichen and there, look, a white spider trying ever so humbly to stay out of sight under a small rock.

Two hours later, we tear ourselves away from a three-metre-square piece of God's earth. Goofball photography with rock-biting lichens – this is a whole new form of tourism.

Further east, growling with an interesting blend of deep diesel and high tenor over the crest of a hill, Jackson Browne and the pick-up take us to a world of jasper-red mountains and the tiny Skeleton Coast Park border post of Springbokwater, where a solitary meerkat stands sentry on a roadside rock.

We arrive at a set of significant crossroads. Going north gets us to Opuwo, the slightly eccentric Himba border town, or to Kamanjab, where our mates Jan and Suzi van de Reep run the nearby Huab Lodge in a conservancy of farms that provides great shelter and protection for some desert-adapted elephants.

A funny thing about elephants. You're up in the Chobe in northern Botswana, and there are so many thousands of them milling about, you long for a sighting of a simple impala. But out here, if you come across even one of those sandy sods, it's like dot balls at the end of an exciting one-day game of cricket – gold dust, in other words.

We haven't seen the Van de Reeps for many moons, but we'll never forget them. Jan, the lanky Dutchman, has a sense of humour perfectly matched to the rocky, mountainous, godforsaken world around him. With Jan, it's all a matter of Huab:

'Would you like a little Chateau de Huab?' – drinking water.

'How's your Huab Devil Chicken tonight?' – good roasted chook.

'Look, it's a Huab Swimmer' – a bug floating in your glass of wine.

'The Huab Doctor blows tonight' – a little breeze arrives one evening.

'Have some Huabdal Pinotage' – and so on…

Suzi, on the other hand, has filled our brains with sensations of an elephant we've never seen, a beautiful fellow called Doetab who wanders the length and breadth of the Huab River with his tribe. She sends e-mails on a regular basis concerning Doetab. The last we heard, Doetab had lost a tusk and was trying to get his new balance right.

Maybe he's related to the infamous Een Tand (One Tooth), a desert elephant that reigned supreme in these parts a century or so ago. Een Tand once chased a farmer up a tree and then trashed his donkey cart just for laughs. The farmer, who had absolutely no sense of humour about this, gathered up a posse of his mates and they went out and shot old Een Tand.

Doetab, however, is currently under the protection of the Huab Conservancy and, it is hoped, will not suffer the same fate as his monotusked historic counterpart did.

We're having all these deep memories over a slightly warm Tafel Lager at the Oasis Bar at these very crossroads. The beer seller, who also runs a nifty tyre-repair business, has checked all the wheels and, regretfully, cannot find a single chink in the rubber. In this part of the world, where every rock in the road wants to eat your tyres, you drive slowly and carefully and prayerfully. Alternatively, you take a lot of spare wheels along for the drive.

We have rarely seen a country as dry as Damaraland. Heat shimmers, as they say, in the distance. On the

Above: The mud-made 'desert adapted' elephant display on the road to Khorixas.

Previous page: Welcome to the stony but warm heart of Namibia's Damaraland.

drive, finally, to Khorixas, we see the kind of moxie you need to survive out here. A Van de Reepism, if you will.

'For Sale – Namibian Stones,' says the handwritten sign outside the makeshift stall in the middle of nowhere. It's a really bold move, this selling of stones in a stony land. We stop at one of these stalls and inspect the wares: crystals, quartz, agates and, yes, semi-precious tyre-shredders. All in good nick.

Now we know we're officially in Damaraland. At the crest of a hill, just to the right, is a lorry tyre lodged in the sand, with a welcome sign painted on it. There's no one in the little office nearby. We drive on, as the geology gets weird on me. Eventually, we come across a light-brown hill, twisted by wind and time and erosion into the Sorting Hat from Harry Potter's beloved Hogwarts School for Wizards. We drive past and utter the word *Hufflepuff* softly under our breath.

Not far from the Sorting Hat is the Meerkat Manneken Pis. It is a giant glass-fibre suricate looking furtively over his shoulder as he appears to be having a roadside wee. And there's the sign to the Twyfelfontein Country Lodge, where we suck up a couple of beers and some very pricey sandwiches and head off to see the famous etchings nearby.

Ten years earlier, I had been here on another safari. We were just about to wander around these 6 000-year-old etchings when someone ran up and announced that there were elephants about. We rushed off to the river in our Land Rover and caught sight of a mother, dad and calf loping off into the dusty distance. We partied all night.

This time, we see a magnificent herd of springbok, maybe 50-strong, flying across the road in leaps and bounds, then calming down on the other side, busying themselves with ear-scratching and vacant gazes into the middle distance. It's all good.

At Twyfelfontein, our guide is Dion So≠oabeb, a young Damara with a degree in Rock Art from South Africa's Cape Technikon.

Twyfelfontein is one of those places a traveller has to see before the lights go out. It's a huge outdoor Bushman exhibit going back six millennia. The ancient etchings in the tumbled sandstone outcrops are of accurately depicted animals, but with often-exaggerated features: a very long and crooked lion's tail, a rhino with elongated horns, here a seal, there a three-headed ostrich. This, explains Dion, is how the Bushman shamans saw the animals when they were in trance state.

Also in the area are the Organ Pipes and Burnt Mountain sites, and in tracking them down we come

across a place called The Penis Garden. But the road to this phallic spot is just too rocky and time is no longer on our side. Maybe leave that for next time. We have to find the Petrified Forest before the sun sets. Whatever happened to lunch time in Khorixas?

Moving right along on the C39, we see desert elephants in the distance. But they seem to be moving at speed through a Damara village. Oh no. Is there a wailing of fearful locals? Is there a trumpeting and a trampling?

Nothing of the sort, as it turns out. Instead, there are a number of finely-crafted, nearly life-size, mud elephants lurking around a collection of huts. These are not our desert-adapted Damara elephants. But they're as near as dammit, and we begin developing a sneaking admiration for these crafty locals. The poet Scully once said something about dry spaces giving birth to genius, and one can see it here on the road to Khorixas.

Ha! There it is. The sign to the Petrified Forest welcomes us. It also promises rock art and welwitschias, a rare deal in these parts. We turn in at the gate, and there seems to be just enough late afternoon sun left to make a decent picture. In the distance is a fellow leaping onto his bicycle and flying down in our general direction.

It's Barnabas the guide: 'The entrance fee is ten dollars,' he says.

I grimace at him and make as if to leave.

'No, wait! Just two minutes up the hill is a male welwitschia and a female welwitschia – and some lovely petrified trees. It's really worth it.'

We get out and trudge up the hill with Barnabas.

But this is nothing like how I remember the Petrified Forest from my 1995 visit. There is, literally, only one petrified sapling up here. And two rather shame-faced *Welwitschia mirabili*. Slim pickings indeed.

'What did you do to the forest?' I want to know.

'This is it,' says Barnabas, ushering me down the hill to a rickety table, where he has, wait for it, Namibian stones to sell me. I like the look of his tiger's eyes, his agates, his amethysts and his various crystals. But the man is a rogue, and I will not pay him another sweet cent. Petrified Forest, my foot.

However, I have trading tobacco on the back seat, a bag of foul-smelling Farmers' Co-op weed that I often use as a room odoriser at various dodgy stops on my travels around southern Africa.

'Wow!' he says, his eyes lighting up when he spies the bag of baccy. 'There's gonna be war at home tonight!'

I take my stones, he takes his tobacco and we both give each other jackal looks that say 'Ha! I have the better of you today'. And Jules and I drive off into the gloaming, eventually coming to an official sign directing me to the official Petrified Forest (now closed), but that's fine, too. Informally, we've had a very good day's drive out here in daft old Damaraland.

– Chris

Left: The 'Sorting Hat' hill, near the western border of Damaraland. **Bottom left:** Petrified 'sapling' used as a tourist attraction **Below:** A welwitschia stands guard on a hill along the road to Khorixas.

Right: Some of Africa's westernmost baobabs are found in Damaraland. **Below:** Lichen on the mountain slopes near the Skeleton Coast. **Bottom right:** *Welwitschia mirabilis* on a hill near Khorixas.

In this part of the world, where every rock in the road wants to eat your tyres, you drive slowly and carefully and prayerfully.

Left: The ancient etchings of Twyfelfontein. **Above:** The view of the valley from Twyfelfontein's hill formation. **Right:** The Organ Pipes rock formations near Twyfelfontein. The Organ Pipes were formed 120 million years ago by rapidly cooling and shrinking dolorite.

Twyfelfontein is one of those places a traveller has to see before the lights go out.

OTJIWARONGO

Cheetah Central

Fast Cat Country

BETWEEN OTJIWARONGO AND THE WATERBERG PLATEAU IN NAMIBIA THERE LIVES A MOST ATTRACTIVE HERD OF GOATS. THEY'RE INTELLIGENT, KIND, VISIBLY AMUSED BY HUMANS, AND ONLY A LITTLE SMELLY.

I met them one afternoon as the sun was going down, turning the plateau and the goats into gold. What a great picture this would make, I thought, grabbing my camera. Totally absorbed in the moment, I crept up and focused on a white goat playing King of the Termite Mound, while a piebald one nuzzled my neck and gently sampled the camera strap.

Suddenly, a blonde 'goat' lying under a bush detached itself from the throng with a snarl, rushed at me, barked twice and stood firm in front of the flock, growling. I backed away slowly. Clearly I had come face to face with the Goat of the Baskervilles …

The goats belong to the nearby Cheetah Conservation Fund (CCF), which uses them to help raise tough predator-chasing dogs – Anatolian shepherds. Caesar, to be fair, was probably their fiercest. The CCF has recently introduced the 6000-year-old Turkish dog breed to Namibia to perform a dual function: by keeping livestock safe from predators, they also eliminate the farmers' urges to kill the predators. The Anatolian shepherd is a dog on the frontline of cheetah conservation.

Life in Namibia is hard on farmers. When it's not drought or poachers hammering their bottom line, cheetahs, leopards or jackals are calling their livestock lunch.

Many farmers became as tough as the land, hardening their hearts against predators, including the endangered cheetahs. Whenever they got the chance, many farmers trapped them, shot them, or even ran them over with their bakkies. These farmers have killed well over 6000 Namibian cheetahs in ten years, and numbers worldwide are now down to less than 12000.

This is a huge drop down from a couple of decades ago, when there were 25000.

Yet around 3000 cheetahs (a fifth of all remaining cheetahs) still live in Namibia, the greatest concentration of cheetahs in the world. But in the first few years of the 21st century the country began to switch from seeing cheetahs as the fastest vermin on earth to marketing Namibia – particularly, the town of Otjiwarongo – as the Cheetah Capital of the world.

This creature, so ridiculously pretty, a feline Marilyn Monroe on speed, has rates of acceleration that would leave a fast car standing – 0 to 96 kilometres per hour in under three seconds.

Most of the time that they're sprinting, they are flying seven metres through the air between strides, touching the earth four times a second. Any further than 400 metres, though, and they have to stop, or they'll overheat.

For reasons that are still a mystery, cheetah numbers plummeted 10000 years ago, possibly right down to a few breeding individuals. The population

Above: Protection for goats – Anatolian shepherds safeguard livestock against cheetahs.

Previous page: Fast cat on the hunt – a cheetah in full stride.

eventually recovered, but the gene pool is still poor, and every single cheetah alive today is at risk of inbreeding.

This is why Namibia is so crucial. It's really down to 1 000-odd Namibian nationals – most of them farmers, since 90 per cent of Namibian cheetahs live on farms – and a handful of foreigners to save a species. Its numbers must be kept sufficiently high to minimise more inbreeding.

Spearheading the handful of foreigners is Laurie Marker, an attractive American, doing precisely what Namibian farmers hate most – coming from another country to tell them how to run their affairs.

Laurie has succeeded because she has human issues so strongly close to her heart. She sees Namibian stock farmers as the true custodians of cheetah, and, as a result, attitudes are changing: 'Conservation is about people, not just animals.' It's this approach that recently won her the *Time* magazine Hero of the Planet award.

Almost all the cheetahs in captivity anywhere in the world (they now number about 1 200) have come from Namibia. But it was Khayam, a cheetah she raised from the time it was a cub, that brought her to the cheetah stronghold of the world: 'I dreamed of releasing her in Africa.'

That came to nought because Khayam, to cut a long story short, could learn how to hunt, but could not learn bush sense.

That's why cheetahs stay with their mothers for so long – there is much to learn about where to live in the bush, how to stash prey, how to avoid running into cheetah enemies like lions.

It was during this 1980s trip, and the following ones, that Laurie became aware that the farmers were killing cheetah like flies: 'Something clearly had to be done to save the cheetah. An organisation had to be formed, but no one was doing it.'

So in 1990, she gave up her prestigious job in Washington and started the CCF.

The distrustful Namibian farmers put her through hell. They thought she cared only for the cheetahs, not for them, and they'd invite her to come and drink tea with them around the carcass of a recently shot cheetah.

Her mascot, cheetah ambassador and good luck charm is Chewbaaka, whose mother and brothers were victims of the farmer–cheetah war. The livestock owner who shot his mother and siblings toyed with the idea of keeping him as a pet for the children, but finally gave him over to Laurie, who then spent an entire month nursing this frail, malnourished, spotted cub back to life.

A French *Star Wars* fan gave the cheetah his name because of his habit of grumbling querulously under his breath when peeved.

Laurie and her team won the farmers over one by one, mostly by taking their concerns very seriously. The farmers had to make a living, and cheetahs were losing them money.

A conversation she'd had with a scientist in Massachusetts came back to her. He had been seeking a solution to a very similar problem in the USA, where farmers were vehemently opposed to the introduction of wolves.

They had tried out the Anatolian shepherd dog to help safeguard the livestock from among the few dozen possibilities and were very impressed with the results.

Laurie and veterinarian-farmer Arthur Bagot-Smith tried it out in Namibia. At six weeks old, the pup is put into the flock of goats it will guard for the rest of its life.

'They bond with whatever you put them in with,' says Laurie. 'Eventually, you've got yourself a goat, or a chicken, or a sheep, or an ostrich, with a big bark.'

The Turkish breed is big and rangy and is hardy in extreme temperatures because of the light, coarse coat that insulates its body. It is perfect for Namibia. Hans Gunther Gartner, a farmer near Otjiwarongo, is a big fan. In his sing-song German accent, he describes the dog as 'very clever and wakey'.

'If you punish him, he takes it hard,' he says. 'You only need to show him once. I used to have heavy cheetah problems, but since we got the dog, no losses.'

Arthur Bagot-Smith has an Anatolian shepherd too. 'Amy is brilliant,' says Arthur. 'If she doesn't come back at night, I know she's with a ewe giving birth, and I'll find her with the lamb in the morning, watching over it.'

Even former president Sam Nujoma, who has a farm near Otavi, has one of these Anatolian shepherds.

Laurie still visits the USA to fundraise every year, and see friends and family, but she could never go back. Her dream is to see cheetahs running free and wild, and there is no other place to do it.

'And you know, if you've got good friends, a Thanksgiving turkey in the desert isn't so bad…'

– Julie

Cheetahs have friends in very high places.

This page: Namibia is the last stronghold of the world's cheetah population. Cheetahs usually attack livestock when there is no wild game available – most of them are found on farm land today. They are capable of accelerating to nearly 100 kilometres per hour in three seconds.

ETOSHA

Jumbo Rules

Down at the Water Hole

IN SEPTEMBER, ETOSHA IS COOKING IN MORE WAYS THAN ONE. THE EARLY SUMMER HEAT SINKS IN, CASTING MIRAGE WAVES ACROSS THE PANS THROUGH WHICH TROOPS OF ANIMALS MAKE CONSTANT ORDERLY TREKS TO THEIR FAVOURITE WATER HOLES. BY NOON, THE WATER HOLES OF ETOSHA RESEMBLE CHAOS TIME AT HOME AFFAIRS AS THE QUEUES MINGLE AND DRINK — A PERFECT HOUR TO BE OUT THERE WITH YOUR CAMERAS.

Before the rains, all life is concentrated around water sources up here. The vegetation is low and sparse after winter, yet the rich mineral content of the soil is transferred to the grass and trees, and shows up in the plump wellbeing of the animals. The zebras have half-grown colts, and many of the springbok calves are just beginning to sprout sharp little horns.

We enter the park from the Okaukuejo side in the south. Our first stop is the sunken Ombika water hole, shimmering in the white calcrete. It's completely surrounded by zebras standing in a striped torpor and lining up to descend into the freshwater spring.

We drive on to Okaukuejo Camp to check into Etosha. At the water hole next to the camp, thousands of springbok file back and forth, a moving mosaic of fawn, black and white. Every now and then a gemsbok paddles out to the middle and stands in a trance, belly wet, bending its masked unicorn head occasionally to suck up the water. Zebras keep cautiously to the margins, dipping their dark muzzles below water level. The kudus stand guard, flinging their spiral horns back and looking about, ears flicking.

Around the water hole the tourists lounge in their dozens, writing postcards and diaries, looking up occasionally at the alarm bray of a zebra, drinking cold water and eating ice creams.

We continue towards our night stop, Halali Camp, slowing down when we see a handful of cars at Nebrownii water hole, just 200 metres off the road. The springbok are gathered in little groups in the dense shade of thorn trees, utterly indifferent to cars passing less than two metres away. We have to weave between quizzical zebras, and then we see what has entranced the other tourists.

Three huge elephant bulls are converging on the water hole, effortlessly putting to flight dozens upon dozens of springbok, gemsbok and zebras. They anoint their massive bodies in the white mud, then stand with heads close together in communion, giving scant attention to the lesser species begging permission to approach the water. They are the silvered giants of Nebrownii — and every animal knows it.

That night, we take sundowners at the Moringa water hole just outside Halali Camp. As dusk approaches, a stroppy, collared, matriarch elephant with a suckling calf paces back and forth, shaking her ears in anger at the unseemly attentions of a too-young bull towards

Above: Overland tourists scanning an Etosha drinking spot for unusual game activity.
Previous page: A diffident herd of black-faced impala await their turn at the water hole.

one of the young females in her herd. He takes one step too close and she roars at him and charges. He retreats and loiters nonchalantly in the bush several hundred metres away, nursing his injured dignity. Satisfied, she takes her calf and shows her where the cleanest water lies, sucking noisily at the spring. The defended virgin comes and leans against the matriarch gratefully. We half-expect to hear upwellings of opera music after all that drama.

The next morning, we visit Salvadora, Charitsaub and Sueda in the dawn light. Red-crested korhaan pose for roadside pictures. A kori bustard on an intense hunt for lizards ignores us in passing. A secretary bird, looking like a lean groundsman measuring out a cricket pitch, strides along parallel to us, searching for snakes to karate-kick to death.

And everywhere along our drive are Burchell's zebras, lit pale gold in the creamy early light. Teenagers are mock-fighting, rearing up, sneaking bites along flanks, sniffing each other's faces and whispering stripy secrets into pricked ears. Others have their heads down, cropping the morning grass with the sap still risen.

At Rietfontein water hole, we watch at least 500 zebras come down to drink, the mares bickering with one another, the colts observing the protocol carefully. The lead stallion of each group pauses in front of his family before proceeding forward, stopping every few metres to check the line of approach and scanning about for predators.

We move on to Goas water hole. Red hartebeest – with all the charisma of hammerhead sharks – mingle with polite black-faced impalas, presidential gemsbok and plump zebras. Over it all, a yellow-billed kite flies off triumphantly with a fat mouse and calls it breakfast. An eland bull stands cautiously in the shade, also watching the animal tableau. The blacksmith plover tink-tinks in the foreground and, at the far side of the water, two gemsbok challenge one another to duels, testing their strength for the mating season.

On our way to Namutoni Camp the next day, the yellow-grassed plains are dappled with little groups of grazing springbok and zebras. A stately silver bull elephant stands solo in the mopane bush, picking out delicious grass tussocks with his trunk and kicking them loose with his feet, putting them into his mouth only after shaking off the dirt. As he crosses the road in front of us he suddenly turns to face us. He flaps his ears once and opens his eyes wide, as if to warn us to stay still and not startle him.

We stop at Kalkheuwel water hole, which is taken over by a breeding herd of elephants at least 40-strong, clustered around the water. The water level is right down after they shower themselves with liberal, lusty sprays.

About 20 black-faced impalas troop slowly towards the water hole, as self-effacing as a drift of autumn leaves, then stand gazing at the elephant and the water wastage in polite consternation. After a short discussion between them, they turn and walk back through the mopane bush the way they'd come, looking like martyred Franciscan penitents – or dismayed water officers.

The next morning we return and see hundreds of guineafowls darting about like animated tea cosies. Behind us in the bush lurk a few hundred zebras, alert in the shade of the mopane, waiting for a signal and shaking their Trojan-helmet manes. It finally comes, and the first assembled troops clatter forward cautiously over the white rocks in single file, led by a battle-scarred stallion. A lone wildebeest joins the zebra patrol for safety, and the water hole disappears in a blaze of black and white stripes.

At Etosha, people are advised not to drive around too much in search of game. Go to the water hole of your choice and the animals will come. At Kalkheuwel, one man reads a newspaper while another couple in a camper van doze off. This is the magic of the water hole. You may come when there is nothing, but soon a yellow-billed kite will fly over on mouse patrol. A cautious kudu will pick its way decorously through the bush. Some crows may begin bickering on a stump. And then the big herds will appear as if from nowhere and drink their fill.

Normally, wildlife is best photographed at the edges of the day, when the light is soft. This is still true of Etosha. In the mornings, the plains are full of grazing animals, the young are at play and the males are already beginning their jousts. But then there's an extra bonus. The rich light endures into the morning heat, when the animals begin moving to water, and you get a different kind of photograph: massed herds in crisp light. In fact, there are chances of good wildlife shots in Etosha all day long. And because the animals are not people-shy, you can get away with something as short as a 300-millimetre lens for full-frame work. Which is not normally the case in most African parks.

We continue to Two Palms, where a lone giraffe drifts across the endless plains towards the water hole. A kori bustard strides past us towards Fischer's Pan and a dozen Namaqua sandgrouse putter about next to the car like clockwork birds, pecking at grass seeds. Four jackals come to play in front of us, grooming one another, rummaging under bushes for unseen beetle snacks. They come so close they have Chris scrambling for the 18–55 millimetre lens.

On the Dik-Dik Drive near Namutoni, we actually encounter the doe-eyed little buck in the bush. It looks like a delicate dassie on stilts, no taller than a blade of winter grass. Then we find an agama lizard, pale and mottled on the calcrete stones. It looks straight up at us with its crazy orange-ringed eyes, standing its ground even with a 105-millimetre macro in its face. And then we glance up at the skies. The muted light has turned the purple-pod terminalias, tambotis, mopanes, ironwoods and red bushwillows into wrought-iron filigreed lace against the stainless-steel clouds. In the early summer season of Etosha, the only limits on photography are your personal levels of energy.

We finally arrive at Namutoni Rest Camp. Fort Namutoni in the fables.

From small beginnings as a rinderpest checkpoint with fancy walls back in the late 1890s, Namutoni was rebuilt into a Rhinelander's fantasy of a colonial fort. But first it had to have its very own siege, and that happened in late January 1904, when more than 500 Ovambo soldiers threatened the lives of those, who numbered only seven, within its crude walls.

It was the Kaizer's birthday. The Ovambos stormed Namutoni with spears and rifles. A furious little battle ensued, leaving many Ovambos dead and wounded outside the fort. Night fell. The seven men slipped away under cover of darkness. They were found by a German patrol and escorted to the safety of Grootfontein.

At dawn, the Ovambos attacked an empty fort, which they trashed anyhow – just to show that there were, in fact, some hard feelings. A year later, the fancy fort was built. Nothing much happened out here until 1915, when South African troops under General Coen Brits took Namutoni.

Some historians record that the South Africans found 2 000 animals, 92 wagons and more than a million rounds of small-arms ammunition in the fort. General Botha regretfully informed General Brits that he and his forces would have to stay at Namutoni for longer than expected.

Brits, rather famously, replied: 'I have captured 10 000 bottles of rum. My men have as much wild beast flesh as they can eat. We are content ...'

– Julie

One water hole, many species: elephant, kudu, zebra and springbok gather en masse during the dry season.

Below: Zebras in an intimate moment at Ombika water hole.
Right: Springbok waiting their turn at the Nebrownii water hole.

Above: A sunset giraffe near Namutoni Camp. **Left:** Giraffes drinking in concert. **Below:** An agama lizard on Dik Dik Drive.

Left: A pied crow airs his views at a water hole. **Below:** A shady spot at Okaukuejo water hole, perfect for game viewing both night and day. **Bottom:** Winter hardwood textures of Etosha.

Around the water hole the tourists lounge in their dozens, writing postcards and diaries, looking up occasionally at the alarm bray of a zebra, drinking cold water and eating ice creams.

Left: Feeding zebras in the early morning grassland near the pan. **Bottom left:** A northern black korhaan patrols the Salvadora area of the park. **Below:** The beloved knee-high dik dik, one of the choice sightings of Etosha.

TREKKING

Into the Dorsland

SOUTH WEST AFRIKANERS

ALL ALONG OUR TRIP THROUGH NAMIBIA, JULES AND I HAD ENCOUNTERED SMALL REMINDERS OF THE VARIOUS DORSLAND TREKS, AMAZING TESTAMENTS TO ENDURANCE, STUBBORNNESS, INNOVATION, STUPIDITY, HOPE AND DESPAIR, ALL IN EQUAL MEASURE. A WELL-PRESERVED WAGON HERE, A SMALL GREEN *KAPPIE* (BONNET) OF A TREKKER-GIRL THERE, A FARM IMPLEMENT, A FAMILY BIBLE, A HUNTING KNIFE AND A GRAVESTONE — THESE WERE ALL SIGNPOSTS TO THE PAST.

When Gert Alberts and his 82-year-old advisor Johannes van der Merwe came up with a plan to lead a smallish group of runaway Transvaal pioneers westwards in 1875, there was no shortage of takers.

Alberts and his company took 50 wagons and more than 1 400 cattle through the Kalahari, right past Lake Ngami and into what is now known as Namibia.

The second convoy was a total disaster. Apparently, Alberts's success inspired the rest of the disgruntled Boers back home, and they took to the desert in great numbers. Nearly 500 people in 128 wagons were just too much of a load for the at-best-marginal Kalahari ecosystem to bear.

Thousands of head of cattle went crazy out there in the desert, clogged up the scant water holes and died in great numbers. The most-often used historical image from that particular disaster was of cattle licking the shiny rims of the wagon wheels, mistaking the sun's reflection for water – the strangest mirage on record.

And as they crossed the Kalahari, the parched travellers would drop off items such as antique furniture and *wakiste* (wagon chests), even abandoning wagons in a bid to lighten their loads. Of course, 'the wily Bushmen' who roamed these vast sands had fat pickings off the embattled Dorslanders. Suddenly, an ostrich egg filled with cool water from God knows where took on immense value, and the bartering was on.

So far, however, no one had died. Alberts, at Rietfontein, was contacted and he rescued a number of the second expedition while others went back to the Transvaal. The Rietfontein group moved up to the Okavango, where malaria began to strike them down. Pretty soon, the death toll reached 200.

Enter Axel Eriksson – trader, collector of specimens, adventurer and soon-to-be philanthropist. Stunned by the misery of these downtrodden people, Axel wrote to the Cape newspapers of their plight.

These reports bred another great story. All of Cape Town was concerned for the Dorsland trekkers (except, maybe, some of Her Majesty's colonial subjects, who probably thought it served the trekkers right for creating such a fuss and running away) and more than 5 000 pounds were raised for the purpose of helping them.

In 1879, two ships, the *Swallow* and the *Christina* (to be entirely fair, they were of British origin), were loaded with rescue supplies for the Dorslanders. They made their way up the west coast to Rocky Point, near Cape Cross on the Skeleton Coast. Landing there was impossible, so they returned to Walvis Bay. Dorslanders, hearing of this great gesture of kindness from the Cape, sent wagons off to Walvis. The goods were picked up and taken all the way back to Etosha – and the *trekgees* (trekking spirit) pumped once more.

Possibly the most colourful account of life in the Dorsland laager was a work of fiction entitled *The Thirstland*, written by prominent South African author W.A. de Klerk.

One of the most evocative parts of De Klerk's description was the way the women worked the hippo carcass after a day's hunting on the Kunene River.

'The prospects were that the great fat-hunger of the Trek would eventually be appeased,' De Klerk writes. 'Under the trees, at roughly constructed tables, the womenfolk stood cutting up hunks of fat into strips, trimming it, washing it all to a shiny whiteness. The young girls carried the strips on wooden trays to sunny flats, setting them out on the grass. There it lay, like snow on the Cape mountains. The Himbas, hacking at the carcasses, fought noisily with each other for choice titbits. The hunters, tired after a hard day's work, sat under the anas [trees]. Clouds of tobacco smoke hung in the lifeless air. There they sat, drinking coffee, cleaning their guns, talking, and ever talking.'

But they had to beware of the crocodiles. One night, young Nellie le Grange of the Dorslanders went swimming up near Swartboois Drift. A juvenile crocodile took her by the leg. Finally, one Cillie van der Walt and some other Dorsland women dragged both Nellie and the crocodile onto a sandbank and threw sand in the big lizard's eyes so it could

release its grip on the girl. Nellie was saved, but the leg was slow in healing.

An interesting character had entered the world of Dorsland trekking by now: William Worthington Jordan, a young man of colour from the Cape.

He won the trekkers' confidence and became their spokesman. Jordan knew all sorts of places and languages, including Portuguese, and interested them in crossing the Kunene and setting up home in Angola. Which they did, from about 1880 onwards. They were now the Angola Boers, living in the Humpata Plateau.

And when the settlers became edgy up on the Humpata, it was Jordan who found them a home back in German West, this time in the Grootfontein area. Although many Boers stayed on in Angola until well into the 20th century, the Grootfonteiners came and set up the short-lived Republic of Upingtonia – a new world for a restless people.

Upingtonia was a complicated place. The local people were opposed to a new state in their midst, and so were both the Portuguese and English colonial powers. What wizardry would these hard-faced Boers be up to now? Bismarck, that 'German of Germans', wouldn't even lend them a little cannon to defend themselves. There were battles with the Herero, the Ovambo and even the Hottentot. Eventually, Jordan was murdered by a prominent Ovambo and the spirit seemed to leak out of the Upingtonia utopia.

But the pioneering spirit of the Dorslanders lives on in modern-day Namibia, mainly in the country's vast farming districts.
– Chris

Previous page: The plains of northern Namibia, once crossed by the desperate Dorsland expeditions.

One of the most evocative parts of W. A. de Klerk's description in **The Thirstland** *was the way the women worked the hippo carcass after a day's hunting on the Kunene River.*

Opposite page – Left: Riverside makalani palm tree. **Right:** Dawn on the Kunene, where many Dorslanders succumbed to crocodile attacks.

This page – Left: The vast dune fields on the Namibian side of the Kunene River. **Bottom left:** Giraffes would have been a regular sight for the Dorslanders on their trek through northern Namibia. **Bottom right:** A Dorsland plaque in the Rietfontein area of Etosha.

DORSLANDTREK
HULDIGINGSFEES
RIETFONTEIN
10-OKT. 1955

Lake Otjikoto

Old Stones

Big Water, Big Rock

LAKE OTJIKOTO — WHICH EXPLORER CHARLES ANDERSSON CALLED 'THAT REMARKABLE TARN' — IS NAMIBIA'S BOTTOMLESS LAKE OF LEGENDS. IN FACT THE BOTTOM HAS BEEN PLUMBED (ESTIMATES OF DEPTH ARE GIVEN AS 50 METRES, 80 METRES AND 120 METRES) BUT THE LAKE REMAINS MYSTERIOUS. JUST THE LOOK OF IT IS ODD — LIKE A DOLOMITIC SINKHOLE FILLED WITH WATER. EXPERTS TODAY AGREE, HOWEVER, THAT AT ONE STAGE OTJIKOTO WAS A HUGE UNDERGROUND CAVE THAT, WELL, CAVED IN.

At the entrance, there was a carving of several faces in a large tree stump, and a large mural of an attractive Herero lady drinking an amber-coloured liquid, with these words next to her: 'Lake Otjikoto Here you are; Touch African curios at the kiosk; Taste sweets, fruit cool drinks and biltong love bites and enjoy Otjikoto.'

An amiable old man who owned the shop, tea garden and strange little garden filled with sundry attractions (parrots, crocodiles and guinea pigs in cages) showed us around briefly. He showed pictures of the cannons that had been hauled from the bottom of the lake (captured from the English by the Germans at the Battle of Sandfontein and tossed by the Germans to the bottom of the lake to avoid their recapture). In 1983 they were pulled to the surface from a depth of 80 metres, perfectly preserved. One man by the name of Tulio lost his hand when the cable hauling a cannon slipped, so the cannon was given his name.

He said the cannons were all at Tsumeb Museum. While we took pictures, a peacock in the parking lot tried its level best to get at the reflection it saw of itself in the windscreen of an old kombi.

At the museum a steady stream of German tourists trickled through the entrance. Apart from the cannons retrieved from Lake Otjikoto, there was an ethnological display of Ovambos, Himbas and Bushmen, and a display of the wide variety of minerals found at Tsumeb, some with exotic names such as dioptase, mimetite, tennantite, wulfenite, aragonite, adamite, cuprite and velvet malachite.

Inside the museum they were selling blue stones (azurite) for several hundred Namibian dollars. The car watchman outside had less-beautiful but nonetheless desirable – and infinitely better suited to our travelling pocket – stones.

We were on our way to see another very large stone – the Hoba meteorite – that fell to earth 80 000 years ago, the biggest meteorite ever to be found intact.

Just before Grootfontein we saw a sign laconically saying 'Meteorite' and followed a long dirt road into the mountains. It went on for so long we thought we must somehow have taken the wrong road, but some extremely friendly farmworkers set us right – it was only three kilometres further on.

We paid our entrance fee and found the meteorite ringed by auditorium seats – as if it was about to give a concert called 'Falling Star'. The meteorite is made almost entirely of metal, mostly iron, with a dash of nickel and cobalt. You could see where determined vandals had tried to chisel away bits of the meteorite, leaving shiny metal exposed. I thought this rather added to the charm of a piece of rock about three metres wide and one metre thick and otherwise rather blockish.

The Hoba meteorite's rivals reside in New York City and in Mexico. In the 1890s, the famed Arctic explorer Admiral Robert Peary brought the Ahnighito meteorite home from Greenland. Peary rather hopefully estimated its mass at 90 tons, but it weighed in at just over 30 – half the size of Aunty Hoba. Next in line is the Bacubirito meteorite of Mexico, weighing 24.5 tons. Many thousands of years ago, a meteorite much bigger than Hoba and her contenders landed in Arizona, but it broke up into little bits. It made an awfully big hole out in the desert, but left very little of itself behind.

'It is all too easy to envy the "Namibians" of the time their good fortune in being spectators to the grand finale of Hoba's space flight,' said Michael Brittan in his book *Discover Namibia*. 'Yet the awesome happenings must have prompted much spiritual supplication among the tremulous populace, to say nothing of the trail of psychological scars which it may have left. It must be remembered that the saga of civilisation still tells of a time when meteorites which fell to Earth were believed to have been sent by the gods.'

Strolling past Hoba without knowing the story, you might not think much of it. To many geologists,

Above: The Hoba Meteorite – the largest intact alien stone to have landed on earth – near Grootfontcin.
Previous page: The legendary bottomless lake near Tsumeb, northern Namibia.

however, Hoba has become something of a Holy Grail, because it comes from *out there*, possibly forged by the early beginnings of our solar system. They say Hoba could well have been a minor planet that suffered a meltdown maybe 300 million years ago, perhaps after a major brush with another planet.   – Chris

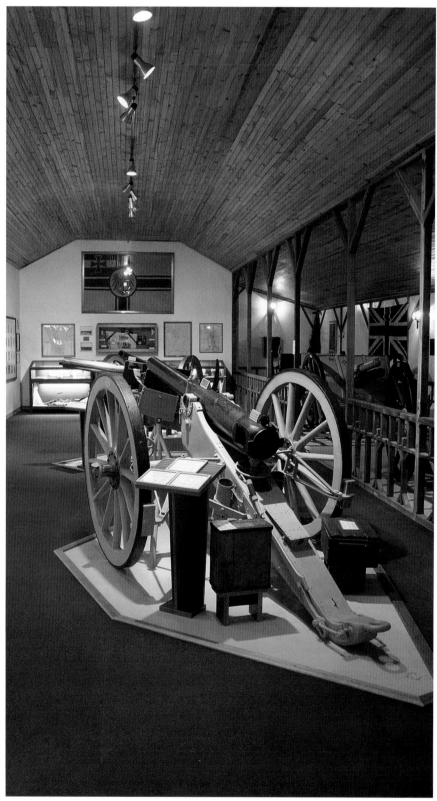

A plaque reading:

JOHANNES STEPHANUS COOK

IN TERE HERINNERING AAN ONS GELIEFDE SEUN
JOHANNES STEPHANUS,
GEB. 16 DES. 1903. TE DE RUST, OUDTSHOORN.
VERDRINK IN DIE OTJIKOTTO MEER. OP 16 OKT. 1927.
TERWYL HY MET VRIENDE GAAN SWEM HET.
SY LYK IS NIE GEVIND NIE.

"DIEPE WYSHEID ZYN U PADEN
WY AANBIDDEN ZWYGEN STIL." GES. 21 vs 4.

DIE TREURENDE OUERS C. EN S. COOK.

Opposite page – Top left: Tsumeb, world famous for its crystal mine. **Bottom left:** Direction to Hoba, the biggest meteorite on earth. **Right:** One of the German cannons recovered from Lake Otjikoto after the First World War.

This page – Above: A slightly damaged spot on the Hoba meteorite where vandals tried to chip away part of it. **Left:** A plaque in honour of one J. S. Cook, who drowned while swimming with friends in the lake.

KAVANGO

Mekoro Sunset

CAPRIVI ROAD

THE FIRST TIME WE MET THE GYPSY CRAFTERS OF KAVANGO WAS IN THE MIDST OF A DUST STORM ON THE B1 BLACKTOP HIGHWAY JUST OUTSIDE THE SOUTHERN HAMLET OF GRÜNAU, HOME OF THE NAMA AND THE BIG SKY. THOMAS KASINDA, SQUINTING THROUGH A WALL OF FINE SAND, TRIED TO FLOG US SOMETHING IN MAHOGANY AND LEADWOOD, A FINE PIECE CUT MANY HUNDREDS OF KILOMETRES AWAY IN THE BORDER TOWN OF RUNDU.

'Where do you stay?' I wanted to know. Thomas and his mates were far from home, on the side of the road in the middle of a Namibian nowhere.

'Here, here,' he pointed at an igloo made of black plastic bags at the back of his stall. 'We work here, we drink here, we sleep here. If it's no good here, we go to Windhoek. Or west, to Swakopmund. And when we have sold our carvings, we jump on the bus and ride north, to Kavango – home…'

And now, finally driving through Kavango after these many weeks of drifting around Namibia, I see why Thomas and the gang travel so far to sell their wares. There's just too much competition on home turf, too much tarmac and too little tourist trade. Just after the makalani palm belt north of Grootfontein, you come to the veterinary disease control point and then you're into Kavango proper. After that, right up to Rundu on the Okavango River, you pass thatched-hut villages, each specialising in one particular craft.

Take David Punga, for instance. He makes large wooden helicopters, aeroplanes and cars. One of his metre-long sedans has a speedometer, which David sets for me at 100 kilometres per hour, and his entire crafting fraternity goes rolling about the white dust in laughter.

We drive on and find Paul Jack the woodcutter. He's carrying an enormous pile of cut branches on his bicycle and wearing no-name shades to ward off the sun reflecting off the white sand.

'We are poor, but we are friendly,' he assures us.

We see more of that ten kilometres on, when we stop at a bottle shop for a cold, refreshing Tafel Lager and a kid comes smiling by on a mekoro canoe dragged by rangy oxen, their hooves pounding away at the dust. I shake my head at the strange sight and vow never to drink beer in the middle of a Kavango day again. But I have made that very promise before – and broken it…

Rundu, when we get there, is the same old cowboy border-town as always. I remember it from another era when white South African men wore brown army uniforms instead of this bright and flapping Hawaiian tourist shirt, these clam-digging khaki quasi-shorts and these rubber sandals. Take note, politicians and military types wherever you may be: it's much more fun invading a country with a camera than with a gun. You also make more friends that way.

Above: David Punga – master crafter of the Great Kavango Road.

Previous page: Fishing for supper in the twilight near the Angolan border.

One remembers Rundu as being a bit of smugglers' town, where certain bigwigs of all hues and persuasions went elephant hunting in attack helicopters and fattened their personal accounts with ivory money. They don't teach you that in military school. It was a Total Onslaught, all right. A Total Onslaught on the environment.

But hey, we're not here for war stories. It's Tourism Boom time for Rundu, and one of the prime establishments in the area is Sarasungu River Lodge, which looks across the drowsy waters at the village of Calai, over in Angola, which used to be famous for its Cuca beer shops and also for its canvas boots – Calai takkies, we called them.

In the evening, with the sun fighting through the haze of early summer bush burns, we cadge a cruise down the river. Two swamp boubous call raucously from the trees, and it looks like all the good citizens of Calai are having a river bath. The kids, heads frothing white with carbolic soap, splash about like African Huck Finns, free and laughing in their birthday suits. How the school-going, more affluent Namibian youngsters on the other side of the water must envy them.

We pass Rundu Beach, which is the launching point for cross-river canoe trade between the two countries. We discover we would need a special visa to visit Calai, while the locals pass to and fro as if it's one country.

'It's a question of security,' says our guide. 'And besides, there are still plenty of unexploded land mines around the village.'

It seems the old days are never too far away, up in the Caprivi...

After many days of Two Minute Noodles and Breakfast Bars, it's better than sex to sink your fangs into a decent T-bone steak with all the trimmings. John Craill, who owns Sarasungu, says we can stay here for the measly sum of R250 a night, with breakfast thrown into the deal. He must be a farmer, I think. No hotelier in his right mind would charge so little for so much.

'I happen to be a farmer,' he assures me. 'But I bought this place for a reasonable price and I don't feel I should rip people off.'

Now this is not the kind of language you normally hear in the hospitality business, so the T-bone just kind of idles there in my gullet for a while as my jaw drops in amazement.

Anyhow, we leave the soft cotton sheets and quality whiskies of Sarasungu River Lodge before dawn the next day to venture into the Caprivi along the Golden Highway. Seeing the various party establishments of Rundu (obviously closed at this hour), I feel a pang of regret and make a mental note to visit Club Serious, Papa Carlito's and Joy World Shebeen the next time I'm in town.

It's the thatch-gathering season, and all along the road there are bundles of good materials for roofing – these are one of Caprivi's main sources of income. The heat is descending in withering waves as we pull in at the Popa Falls. The guide books have told me the falls are no great shakes but one doesn't care. There must be liquid, especially of the cold, amber, frothy variety.

I'm in luck. A jovial receptionist/barman takes our ten-dollar entry fee, sells us a brace of Tafels with beads of sweat on the flanks and leans back in his air-conditioned comfort zone, swivelling his eyes back on the satellite-TV soccer game. This guy has the best job in southern Africa, I'm thinking right now. Does he have the faintest idea of how damn hot life is out there?

The Caprivi National Park does not yield much in the way of Kruger-type eye candy yet. That's because all God's animals in the region still have to step daintily around the landmines that the war years left behind – and then face the odd poacher's gun to boot. But that will come with time.

At Kongola, we meet Lance Young of Susuwe Island Lodge, our home for the next two nights. I'm not keen to leave our bakkie out here for 48 hours (What do you expect of a Jo'burg boy?), so he says 'OK, follow me through the sand.'

Sailing along (literally), I drive past the old South African Defence Force base called Fort Doppies. I stifle a giggle as a memory returns of an erstwhile South African Minister of Police who came out here once on a junket and was surprised on the bush toilet by the camp lion. But nothing remains of Fort Doppies except for the memories that people still drag out in the wee hours when the whisky bottle lies low...

We cross the Kwando River to the island of Susuwe and into a world of carmine bee-eaters and their white-fronted brethren. At the lodge, each room has a plunge pool outside, where you can park and watch firefinchs, waxbills, crakes and squirrels compete for the seeds and water on the deck.

The evening cruise on the clear Kwando is magical. With a sunset drink in hand, one listens to the river practically purring with joy. Reed frogs twitter, fish splash, a bat whirrs by and there, not too far away, comes the chortling honk of a hippo. You are so far away from the world here. There's not a taxman, cold-caller or deadline in sight.

The Two Minute Noodle Kids get fried Brie, delicious kingklip and chocolate mousse for supper, and at dawn they're back among the papyrus, waking up the hippos and waiting for the sun. Brunch back at the lodge is a feta omelette and a smoked-beef salad taken next to a massive sausage tree while a collared sunbird sips nectar from one of its maroon flowers.

The afternoon drive with Lance takes us to the Horseshoe part of the Kwando, where we visit a tribe of baboons and then watch a very wary herd of Angolan elephants come to drink. Having dodged poachers and antipersonnel mines to get here, they're in no mood for bonding with humans. We keep our distance, and fix long lenses.

At supper, lodge manager Clinton Edwards talks of the lodge's links with the local community. More than 200 of its staff come from the area and guests pay towards a well-monitored community chest, which has built a school and a water pipeline so far.

'We are talking about establishing a village for tourism and crafts, which will also be supported by other lodges in the area,' says Clinton. 'Tourism is starting to make an impact here.'

We're on the road to Katima Mulilo which, I now discover, is not really the end of the gnarly old geo-finger they call the Caprivi Strip. You actually have to leave Namibia for a while, drop through the Chobe and come in again at Kasane. From there, you cross the border and head for Impalila Island Lodge which, officially, still lies in Namibia.

– Chris

Left: Evening activities on the riverside at Calai Village, Angola. **Below:** Bream fishing on the Kavango River.

EASTERN CAPRIVI

One Island, Four Countries

Wings over Africa

'HAPPY DAYS,' SAID COLIN BRISTOW AS HE PASSED ME THE AIRSICK BAG AND FLEW INTO A CLOUD SOMEWHERE OVER ZIMBABWE.

I was temporarily insane. Who the hell else chugs heavy antimalaria tablets with a half-bottle of home-grown tequila, scoffs a serious airport breakfast and goes flying in a little Cessna 210 at noon, when there's nothing up there but tatty modern-day pterodactyls, bad-news thermals and a Zim pilot with evil intentions?

This was January, the Deadbeat Season from the Delta to the DRC, when mosquitoes rule and electric storms light up the skies all along the Caprivi Strip. High on tequila afterburn and psychotic from the medication, I waived the barf-bag option and concentrated on the Marabou Circuit Court outside my window. The storks looked like ruffled old Supreme Court judges waiting for the jury. I felt like a convicted man serving out his sentence.

I hardly noticed the Victoria Falls below, the subsequent landing or being led to my room at Impalila Island Lodge at the very end of Namibia. I remember wanting to throttle an English tourist somewhere between the customs hut and the horizon for some nefarious reason – nothing else. That night, in a sweat bath, I dreamt of elephants dancing the Macarena in Nike takkies, giraffes with long cocktail glasses and sunbirds with cummerbunds. Sorry ma, the muti made me do it.

Dawn brought a measure of sanity and a fishing expedition. Colin Bristow and ranger Hayden Willans seemed to troll half the Zambezi, to no avail. Sometimes the tiger would sneak up and snaffle the bulldog bait, other times there would be great excitement as the line snagged on a branch and the tension mounted. We chugged back to the lodge and took refuge in a cup of tea while Hayden messed about in the shallows with his rod. Within minutes he had caught a teenage tiger fish and its more respectably sized uncle.

'You should see them when the storms come,' said the lodge manager, Simon Parker. 'The water boils with tigers eating the baitfish eating the insects.'

He told me the Kahuna of all Zambezi tiger fish lived up the river and took your line, your bait and your self-respect without ever showing himself.

'Some call him the Steam Train. Others call him the Pig with Fins.'

I wanted to know how such a superb island lodge could exist out here, with nothing but sneaky finger-biting fish and Lozi people on mysterious *mekoro* (dugout canoes) missions for company.

'Meat comes in from Namibia, fuel from Botswana, dry goods, fruit and veggies from South Africa,' he said. 'You deal with trucks, flights, border posts and VAT – running supplies into this camp is a matter of genius.'

I still had mild antimalarial hallucinations on the evening cruise along the Chobe River, so I shut up and watched a huge family of querulous jumbos cross the river like the Lost Patrol, fish eagles posing like painter's models on dead branches, skimmers, squacco herons, open-billed storks and the ubiquitous marabous striding along the banks on their tatty old legs.

'They might look clumsy on the ground, but you should see them soaring through the air,' someone said. Yeah, right. Like that Circuit Court mob from yesterday, being tumbled to all corners of the sky...

Interesting fellow, Colin Bristow. A 47-year-old Bulawayan with a charming wife called Sharon and a delicious little baby girl called Isobel, Bristow is part of an elite breed of African bush pilots who only need 600 metres of clear landing strip and a G&T before supper to make them happy.

In that first day of delirium, I noted: 'It's the easy familiarity with Africa, the can-do approach of the bush pilot whose little Cessna can land practically anywhere, bearing women, clients, liquor, groceries, gifts, friends and news from afar. It's the lifeline to thousands of people working the lodges from that side of the Atlantic to this side of the Indian. There's a kinship between Colin Bristow and the lodge staff. He is familiar with guiding, has a vast knowledge of the bush, a sense of purpose and seems to know the human condition quite well. It's the pilot we all turn to in times of stress and emergency – he and the game ranger have taken the place of the Great White Hunter in New African Tourist Mythology.'

Of course, Bristow would deny every word...

We flew west along the Caprivi with the Chobe to the left, the Zambezi to the right and a vast flood-plain system below. I'm an old, flea-bitten road-hack, but I was fast becoming a fly-in safari fan. It cuts all the small print and trail dust out of an African trip, especially for those poor Americans who only have two weeks of annual leave. We landed at the Immelman Strip more than a 100 kilometres west of Katima Mulilo, and I had a scary flashback to 1972, when I was drafted for national service and ended up killing

Above: Baby baboon along the Kwando River.
Previous page: The centre of Impalila Island Lodge – a giant baobab.

time in these parts. Now I was back, visiting a smart game lodge called Susuwe – ain't life strange?

Susuwe Island Lodge lies on Birra Island in the Kwando flood plain within West Caprivi National Park which, for the interested ones, lies in the Greater Bambwata Conservancy. It's remote, it's creatively designed and the plunge pool outside each unit comes with a personal stamp of approval from the author. Here, I met Rolf 'Tie Me Kangaroo Down' Harris and we went into a photo frenzy together at a hippo pool, trying to capture that moment just after the big toothy yawn and the nervous dash back to the vehicle.

That's the thing with hippos, I find. One minute they look like your best mate's highly strokable Staffie with their backlit little ears, the next they're out there and at you, earning their living being the most dangerous animals in Africa.

The next morning Bristow the Bush Pilot became Bristow the Bush Guide and we followed a metre-wide trail made by elephants on Kalahari sand through huge teak forests and into spreads of silver cluster-leaf *Terminalia*. We walked in a loop and Colin did a bit of 'client management' by judging that, in the growing heat, I would find an hour of this interesting. Anything more and I would have called in a medevac chopper.

He suddenly stopped at a clearing, made a call like a pearl-spotted owl and had himself a bird party. Six types of very angry birds converged on Bristow the Faux Owl, determined to drive him from their nests. I was gobsmacked – but then, in the company of this mad Zimbo, one often gets like that. The man is full of surprises.

Now we were heading down into Botswana, backtracking via a befuddling route of border posts, but I didn't mind. Bristow's little Cessna had become my nest and we were flying in the quiet of the early morning with no hangover nor malaria muti in the bloodstream. It's heaven, as you hang out up there, seeing the Big Picture of the best continent on earth.

'I'll be back – no tequila, no meds next time,' I assured Colin Bristow, as we took our leave at Bulawayo Airport.

'Happy days,' he replied with a smile, and wandered off to refuel his magical Cessna.   – Chris

African rush hour: A bush pilot flies over the Zambezi as the mekoro man crosses the river in the early morning.

Left: Riverside grooming session for young baboons. **Bottom left:** Whimsical and charming décor detail at Susuwe Island Lodge. **Below:** Southern carmine bee-eater at home on the banks of the Kwando.

Left: Traditionally harassed and hunted by poachers from both sides of the border, a herd of nervous Caprivi elephants comes to drink in the early evening. **Top right:** Water lilies surround Susuwe Island Lodge, dream escape on the Caprivi Strip. **Bottom right:** Hippo rule the reed channels along the Kwando River.

Left: White-fronted bee-eater, one of the many residents of Susuwe Island.
Bottom left: Papyrus lines the Kwando River. **Below:** A shy lechwe ram in his swampy kingdom.

That's the thing with hippos, I find. One minute they look like your best mate's highly strokable Staffie with their backlit little ears, the next they're out there and at you, earning their living being the most dangerous animals in Africa.

𝓘NDEX

BIBLIOGRAPHY

Brittan, M. *Discover Namibia*, Struik, Cape Town, 1979.

Bulpin, T.V. *Discovering South Africa*, Tafelberg, Cape Town, 2001.

Craven, P. and the Namibian National Biodiversity Task Force, ed. Barnard, P. *Biological Diversity in Namibia*, Namibian Directorate of Environmental Affairs, Windhoek, 1998.

De Klerk, W.A. *The Thirstland*, Middlesex, Penguin, 1979.

Green, L.G. *So Few Are Free*, South Africa, Howard B. Timmins, 1946.

Green, L.G. *Lords of the Last Frontier*, South Africa, Howard B. Timmins, 1952.

Green, L.G. *On Wings of Fire*, South Africa, Howard B. Timmins, 1967.

Seely, M. *The Namib: Natural History of an Ancient Desert*, Windhoek, Shell Namibia, 1987.